Drink as Much as You Want And Live Longer

The Intelligent Person's Guide to Healthy Drinking

Drink as Much as You Want And Live Longer

The Intelligent Person's Guide to Healthy Drinking

by Fred M. Beyerlein

Loompanics Unlimited
Port Townsend, Washington

This book is sold for informational purposes only. Neither the author nor the publisher will be held accountable for the use or misuse of the information contained in this book.

Drink as Much as You Want and Live Longer:
The Intelligent Person's Guide to Healthy Drinking
© 1999 by Frederick M. Beyerlein, MBA, MS, CNSD, RD

Published by:
Loompanics Unlimited
PO Box 1197
Port Townsend, WA 98368

Loompanics Unlimited is a division of Loompanics Enterprises, Inc.
1-360-385-2230
E-mail: loompanx@olympus.net
Web site: www.loompanics.com

Cover design by Linda Greer

ISBN 1-55950-188-X
Library of Congress Card Catalog 98-88183

Contents

About the Author

Fred Beyerlein, a nutritionist, serves as Nutrition Services Manager at Sutter Medical Center in Sacramento, California. He has taught at the college level and worked in a hospital-based alcohol and substance abuse program. He has been a guest speaker at various seminars and for corporate wellness programs, and is frequently interviewed by news stations on nutrition. Mr. Beyerlein has also published research in the national publication *Dietetic Currents*.

Important Note to the Reader

The nutritional supplementation program outlined in this book is based on the education, personal, and professional experiences of the author. Because each person has his or her own biochemical individuality and medical history, the author recommends that the reader check with a qualified health professional to determine if there is an underlying medical condition that would prohibit the use of the information in this book. The author knows of no one who has been adversely affected by drinking healthier.

Acknowledgments

To everyone I ever shared a drink with, especially my best friends Mike, Vinny, Jeff, Sandy, Jim, and Fred who were kind enough to take part in my earliest drinking healthier experiments during college. To Martin who gave wise counsel. To my parents who taught me to respect alcohol and always had a good stock of liquor in the house. (Dad, can you pick up another bottle of 30-year old Scotch?) Finally, and most importantly, to Cindy who believed, motivated, and encouraged me to package my thoughts for all to read. All my love is yours, without you this book would never have been completed.

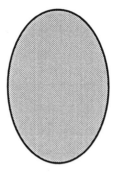

Introduction
by Baxter Slate, R. Ph.

"Booze and reds don't mix son, and I've seen ya take 'em both at once" — Drinker of the 20th century, "Spermwhale" Whalen, The Choirboys

What most people know about drinking alcohol is a haphazard mixture of poorly understood personal experience, folklore, anecdotes, and pseudoscience. Frederick M. Beyerlein's new book does an excellent job of correcting this sorry state of affairs with good advice based upon good science.

Why has there been such a terrible lack of correct and helpful information about drinking? There are several reasons. First and foremost is that alcohol is a drug and falls into the same category as other vices and is therefore demonized. The United States in particular has had a profound love-hate relationship with alcohol, the most spectacular example being the enactment of the eighteenth amendment to the Constitution — Prohibition. The complete ban on beverage alcohol went into effect on January 16, 1920. The law was in effect for thirteen years until another Constitutional amendment was passed that repealed prohibition. A simple study of American history will immediately reveal how divisive this governmental policy was for all Americans. The phrase "the roaring '20s" does not refer to the economy of the times as much as it does the staccato sound of the Thompson submachine gun, a prized weapon of bootleggers. As a result of rampant homicide and interstate liquor trafficking, police powers were stepped up, particularly for the FBI.

Regardless if one obeyed the law and did not drink or whether one broke the law and imbibed, the message behind the law was clear: drinking alcohol was an absolutely abhorrent thing to do. Even if one tippled on occasion and created no ill consequences for himself or others, he had to rationalize breaking the law. This is an easy thing to do for real criminals. For ordinary law-abiding people just the notion in the back of the mind of being a "law-breaker" is enough to cause mental discord if not outright anxiety.

Today alcohol is legal but we still face the same governmental and social demonization as in prohibition but with strange twists and turns. Laws keep being enacted to "crack down" on alcohol use. But now laws are enacted piecemeal rather than a complete prohibition. For many years the individual states were allowed to set the minimum age for drinking. The federal government wanted the minimum age set at 21. The feds did not want to become embroiled in a "state's rights" issue so they took a " back-door" approach. They threatened to cut off federal matching highway funds unless all states set the drinking age at 21. No state wanted to go without the funds or fight the feds so all states complied.

Another form of governmental crackdown on alcohol currently in vogue is to step up the penalties for drunk driving. While this sounds like a good move to reduce drunk-driving collisions and fatalities the reality of the situation is more complex. Many drivers arrested for drunk driving are not problem drinkers or abject alcoholics. Revocation of their driver's license, jail time and huge fines may be much more harmful to the individual than any "threat" the driver created for himself or others while driving intoxicated. Stiffer penalties do little to keep the truly dangerous alcoholic drivers off the road because they usually keep on driving whether or not they have a valid driver's license!

One of the easiest ways to crack down on intoxicated drivers is simply to lower the BAL (blood alcohol level) that constitutes "drunk driving". The police are unbelievably imaginative when it comes to finding a reason to stop a motorist. One whiff of alcohol on your breath and you will be performing a field sobriety test in no time. You may have been driving more alertly and carefully than 80 percent of the people on the road but if you blow more than 0.08 (or whatever the current standard) you will spend the night in the slammer.

Suppose that you have been convicted of or have pled guilty to a crime that took place while you were under the influence of alcohol.

The new judicial trend is for the courts to impose a two-fold sentence. One for the crime itself, say DUI or domestic violence, and another for "alcohol treatment" or perhaps "alcohol education." You may be placed under a court order to take a drug (usually Disulfiram) on a daily basis to prevent you from drinking. This drug works by incapacitating the complete metabolism of alcohol so that a toxic waste material called acetaldehyde builds up and in theory makes you very ill if you imbibe. This daily tablet taking ritual usually takes place in a pharmacy and can be humiliating if you encounter a self-righteous "clean and sober" pharmacist.

Whether or not you go to an Alcoholics Anonymous meeting voluntarily or by court order, you will be presented with a belief system that is Christian in nature and gives no other alternative to problem drinking than total abstinence. AA devotees will argue the point about Christianity and call your salvation "belief in a power greater than yourself." I need only quote from the chapter in the official AA manual entitled "Doctor Bob's Nightmare". Doctor Bob's short story of his recovery from alcoholic abasement ends with the upbeat admonishment "Your Heavenly Father will never let you down." Must one become a Christian to stop drinking?

Even if one does not enter a treatment program under court order one is likely to be spending a huge amount of money for "rehab." One is likely to be exposed to the same kind of indoctrination as in AA but with an emphasis on a "twelve-step program." I have often wanted to personally congratulate the natural scientist who discovered the arcane fact of the universe that exactly twelve steps, not thirteen, not seven-and-a-half, but twelve, is the exact number of steps needed to achieve sobriety! It does not take an Oliver Stone to figure out that twelve is the number of sycophants that a certain Jew who lived 2,000 years ago had in his posse. One of the key tenets of all these group meetings is the idea of denial. While it is surely the case that some people are truly in denial about many undignified facts about themselves, the argument form about others being in denial is, in logical terms, a circular argument.

To try to illustrate this suppose that two people have a difference of opinion about a matter of fact. Roscoe says the earth is shaped like a bag with two walnuts inside. Sam says it's shaped more like a cue ball. If Roscoe and Sam are rational they both present facts that support their own claim and dispute the other's claim. In an ideal world one of them will eventually be persuaded by the reality of publicly verifiable facts and logic. But suppose Roscoe says to Sam that Sam can't accept the reality of the "nut-bag" world because Sam's very belief in a spherical world prevents him from knowing the truth. Essentially Sam is put in a no-win situation; whatever he says Roscoe still counters by saying that it's all invalid because Sam still believes in a spherical world.

While on the surface this argument may seem like no more than a lesson in logic, it does explain the problem with "denial." You could be in four possible situations; 1. You are an alcoholic and admit it. 2. You are an alcoholic and deny it. 3. You are not an alcoholic and say so. 4. You are not an alcoholic but claim you are.

If you are in treatment it is assumed by everyone around you that you are an alcoholic. If you admit you are an alcoholic you are now in their thrall and you will do the twelve steps or else. If you say you are not an alcoholic then you will immediately be accused of being an alcoholic "in denial." If you believe you are not an alcoholic that belief alone will indicate a symptom of alcoholism! It is in many ways similar to early American witch trials; the alleged witch would be tortured up to and including death in an attempt to coerce a confession. If the subject confessed then of course it proved she was a witch. If the subject did not confess she would be tortured to death, a sure sign of a pact with Satan so strong that the witch could resist such super-human torture!

Now with the good news. Most people who drink enjoy drinking. Many people have guilty feelings about drinking and see it as a vice. They also may feel shame and remorse about it. From all of the previous information presented it is easy to see how one can form guilty feelings about drinking due to powerful governmental and social pressures. This book is a breakthrough in the sense that it gives an objective assessment of what can be done to minimize the risks associated with drinking. If one knows that one is behaving in a reasonable and rational way then one should not feel guilty about doing it.

If you drink, this is a book to be taken very seriously. For if you follow the reasonable and well-researched guidelines you can start taking much better care of your body. Hopefully you will be able to stop feeling guilty about doing something you enjoy and begin to drink free from doubt and physical detriment. *Bon appetite!*

Preface

The great pleasure in life is doing what people say you cannot do — Walter Bagehot

Seven drinkers just finished their last drink of the night and make their way to seven different residences.

Carl is a 44-year-old manager who just came home from a wedding reception. Being an occasional drinker, Carl had three drinks. Two more than usual. Carl thinks the reason he always develops a hangover is that his tolerance to alcohol is low. Little does Carl know the hangover is due to eating too much of the wrong foods before, during, and after drinking. He knows he will have a hangover in the morning. Thank goodness tomorrow is Sunday, and not a work day.

Tom is a 19-year-old college student who survived a campus party that served a grain-alcohol based slush punch. Tom drank two super-sized servings of this icy treat. The fact that this might be a nightly occurrence, coupled with a chips-and-pizza diet, leaves Tom's body with little hope of replacing his life-force vitamin, mineral, and anti-oxidant stores. Unfortunately, in the life of a college student, Sundays are not a day of rest. Another party, and a late night study session with an assortment of junk food is par for the course. Tom is relying on the recuperative powers of youth, but when they're gone, what will Tom have to depend on?

Denise is a 36-year-old marketing executive who just finished entertaining a new client. Denise consumed five vodka martinis during the evening. Denise subscribes to the one-meal-a-day program of dieting. She is disciplined and eats very low-fat foods. Although she regularly exercises and does not have an extra ounce of body fat, her life-force vitamins, minerals, anti-oxidants, and cellular water are not being replaced due to her restricted food intake. Moreover, Denise looks older than her years and frequently catches the flu. Denise finds it harder to recuperate from a night of drinking, and uses all day Sunday to rest.

Steve is a 37-year-old sports fan who just witnessed the most depressing scene ever at Candlestick Park. The San Francisco Forty-Niners were blown out by the North Carolina Panthers 44-3. Steve is going to bed with a stomach bloated with hot dogs, chips, nuts, and 96 ounces of beer. Steve works on Sunday mornings, but he will be calling in sick tomorrow.

Linda is a 56-year-old sales clerk who drinks almost every night at the neighborhood bar. She is a regular drinker, but not an alcoholic. Tonight she enjoyed her usual six Beefeater Gin and tonics. At a routine physical her doctor told her to cut back on her drinking. Her liver enzymes were elevated, indicating liver damage. The doctor will check her enzymes again in three months. The doctor tells her the doom and gloom of cirrhosis of the liver. However, the doctor offers no usable information that would allow Linda to drink healthier.

Joe is a 25-year-old landscaper who just closed up the Oasis, a nightclub he frequents each weekend, which is the only time he drinks. Joe had six shots of tequila and five beers tonight, a little less than some weekends. Drinking increases Joe's appetite. He had breakfast at a diner where he really put away the bacon and sausage before heading home. Joe works out with weights and runs three times a week. Often Joe is told to stop drinking in order to lose his "beer" belly. The truth is Joe's "beer" belly is really a "fat" belly from eating too late, and not from drinking too much.

Bill is a 64-year-old retired county worker. Bill is an alcoholic. He knows it. It doesn't bother him. He doesn't bother anyone either. He just drinks his days away. Everyone tells him to quit drinking. Bill believes this is not possible; so do the people who tell him to quit drinking. Bill lives alone and eats mostly canned food. His diet has very little protein and usually is high in fat. Bill's family and doctor have been telling him for years to quit drinking. During all those years his health steadily declined, but nobody knew how to teach Bill to drink healthier.

Any of the above people could be your wife, husband, lover, friend or family member. If they knew how to drink healthier, they could take specific steps before, during, and after drinking to minimize the damage that alcohol can inflict in terms of lowered immunity, premature aging, and organ dysfunction. What's more, they would feel better the morning after and would not need to miss work or spend the day nursing their wounds. What if you could learn a way to drink healthier?

What if you could teach a drinker to drink healthier? Forget for a moment why he or she drinks or that you may be against drinking entirely. What if you had the power through the knowledge of this book to positively affect your health or the health of someone you love? Would you? Of course you would. I have taught hundreds of people to drink healthier. If I had a son or daughter going to college, I would not be so naïve as to think that he or she will not drink. I would not take the chance. I would give life-force nutrients: anti-oxidants, lipo-tropic factors, vitamins, minerals, and herbs, and information about protein and water needs. Then if he or she decides to drink, he or she would be prepared. Fast paced lives, old age, or youth are no excuse for ignoring the damage alcohol can cause. I define the above nutrients as life-force nutrients be-cause their presence protects the liver and other tissues from alcohol damage, and their absence or insufficient presence swings open a door that leads into a world of debilitating health problems. *Drink as Much as You Want and Live Longer* provides drinkers of all ages, lifestyles, and levels of consump-tion with a plan that protects their health. From a societal standpoint, it is far less costly to have informed drinkers rather than uninformed.

This book is not meant to encourage drinking. Its message is simple. If you drink, I can teach you to drink healthier. The point is not arguable. A 21st Century Drinker can live longer and incur fewer alcohol-related health problems when com-pared to an undernourished counterpart. A 21st Century Drinker is defined as an individual who has optimal life-force nutrient stores. Drinking is a personal decision. If you decide to drink, you should learn how to drink healthier.

People have been drinking alcohol for at least 5,000 years. Benjamin Franklin once said, "God loved us so much that He

created alcohol because He likes to see us happy." This is veri-
fied in the Bible, for it states that God created everything. The
restaurant and bar industry verifies it also by designating 4
p.m.-7 p.m. as happy hour. Moreover, alcohol in all its splendid
forms has transformed many a down-trodden soul into the life
of the party. Alcohol to many people is liquid happiness.

Let's not be naïve: people are social animals, and they are
the only animals that drink when they are not thirsty. I would
bet my liver that as long as there are people on this planet, and
fermentable carbohydrates (sugar), there will be alcohol consumption. Some people drink now and then while others drink
until it kills them. And it too often does. Alcohol does not discriminate against the user. Everyone is invited and treated to
the same dose of euphoria. No matter how much or how little
you drink, alcohol is treated by the body as a toxin. As your
body clears the alcohol from the blood, the body is drained of
its life-force nutrients. These nutrients are needed to neutralize
alcohol, and perform literally hundreds of metabolic reactions
necessary to maintain a healthy body. Adequate cellular water
is essential for transporting nutrients inside the body and for
waste elimination. Anti-oxidants prevent free-radical damage
and premature aging, and lipotropic factors and herbs cleanse
the liver and a help repair damaged cells. The more you drink,
the more life-force nutrients are lost or destroyed. Without
adequate replacement the body becomes sick.

Luckily, science has revealed the path alcohol takes once you
swallow it. The vitamins, minerals, lipotropic factors, cellular
water, and anti-oxidants destroyed or lost during the body's
battle with alcohol are known. This book can teach you to
strategically replace these life-force nutrients. What's more, it
will teach you how to use life-force nutrients to protect the
body during future indulgences, much like a condom is used to

protect against disease and unwanted pregnancy. However, there are people against the idea of providing condoms to high school students. These people are against the idea of rampant teenage sex outside the marriage bed. However, we all know that teenage sex is going to happen because teenagers are young adults. Like adults, they too are the only animal that mates all year round! Clearly, the provision or exclusion of condoms will not change this immutable fact, or the desire of a teenager to experiment with sex.

Likewise, just as there are people who are against providing high school students with condoms, there are people against the idea of providing a drinker with information that can enable the drinker to drink healthier. The people who are against the idea of drinking healthier are against the idea of drinking under any circumstances. Even though the use of life-force nutrients can prevent human suffering, they would rather have the "sinner" or "weak" person suffer the consequences of the decision to drink. They want nothing short of total abstinence. These people do not want you to have the option to protect your health or the health of someone you love. It's their way or no way.

I encounter this type of individual from time to time. However, after getting the person to put aside their philosophical opposition to drinking healthier, he or she agrees with the idea.

It's worth repeating here: The more you drink, the more you need supplemental life-force vitamins, minerals, anti-oxidants, lipotropic factors, herbs, protein, and water replacement. I mentioned earlier that alcohol does not discriminate. However, the health-care profession does. They discriminate against the drinker when the only recommended treatment is the canned advice "quit drinking" and "attend an Alcoholics Anonymous (AA) Twelve-Step program," knowing full well that the drinker will continue to drink and become progressively more debilitated.

Health professionals should view health problems caused by drinking in the same way as the problem of lactose ingestion in the lactose intolerant person. A lactose intolerant person cannot digest milk sugar because he lacks the necessary enzyme required for its digestion. When he consumes milk or other dairy products he experiences abdominal bloating, gas, pain, and diarrhea. Does the health professional recommend eliminating milk and dairy products from the diet? No. Instead, she recommends that the individual try dairy products in small amounts, use Lactaid enzymes, drink Lactaid milk, or take calcium supplements. The recommendations enable the individual to protect his bones and enjoy dairy products. Why isn't this type of critical thinking applied to the issue of drinking?

When someone is taking the drug Lasix, a diuretic used to achieve fluid balance, she loses massive amounts of potassium into her urine. Therefore, her physician writes a prescription for potassium, too. Why isn't this type of critical thinking applied to the issue of drinking?

This book will teach you how to stay healthy throughout a lifetime of drinking, no matter what your consumption level. I truly believe that by following the steps toward drinking healthier, you will begin on a new journey of self-awareness. The initial steps are so self-nurturing that your body and mind come back into balance with each step taken. This information may never be offered by physicians because they feel it might be interpreted as condoning drinking. Moreover, many physicians know little about nutrition's role in alcohol metabolism and preventive care. In my eleven years as a registered nutritionist, I have seen too much focus placed on abstinence and not enough on the fact that you can drink healthier. The 21st

Century is upon us and it's high time everyone who drinks becomes a 21st Century drinker. So get comfortable, get a drink,
and start drinking healthier.

How Alcohol Depletes Your Life-Force Nutrients

I have taken more out of alcohol than alcohol has taken out of me — Winston Churchill

A Nutritionist's Approach to Drinking Healthier

The internal war of alcohol metabolism has many casualties in terms of nutrient loss. I define some nutrients as "life-force" since their presence protects the liver and other tissues from alcohol damage, and their absence or insufficient presence threatens the drinker's health and quality of life. Clearly, all nutrients are necessary for good health. However, the following life-force nutrients are required to process alcohol and repair damage caused by alcohol and its byproduct acetaldehyde.

Life-Force Nutrients

- Anti-oxidants (cell defenders): vitamins C and E, selenium, and glutathione
- Lipotropic factors (fat burners): carnitine, methionine, cysteine, and lecithin
- Minerals (activators): zinc, magnesium, calcium and phosphorus
- B-Complex vitamins
- Protein
- Water
- Fiber

The following herbs or botanicals are also life-force nutrients since they prevent liver "constipation" by facilitating bile release, a liver cleansing action. Moreover, they help protect and heal damaged liver cells, promote new liver cell growth, and strengthen the immune system which is under attack when alcohol is present.

- Milk thistle
- Dandelion root
- Artichokes
- Goldenseal
- Echinacea
- Cayenne pepper

Drinking healthier will require you to learn how to be a 21st Century Drinker. By strategically combining the life-force nutrients in the correct dosages, you can reduce free-radical damage and organ dysfunction, boost your immunity, prevent hangovers, and slow the aging process initiated by alcohol.

If We Can Sunbathe Healthier,
We Can *Drink Healthier!*

Drinking healthier is a responsible pursuit no different than sunbathing healthier. Both are pleasant activities that carry their own risks and benefits. Alcohol can damage every cell inside the body and the sun can damage your skin. Drinkers can develop alcohol-related health problems ranging from increased susceptibility to colds and flu to cirrhosis of the liver — a disease in which the liver becomes fatty, greasy, and scarred, and which kills 100,000 people each year. Sunbathers can develop damage such as sunburn, premature aging, wrinkling, and skin cancer. However, drinking and sunbathing both can be beneficial. Moderate drinking can protect your heart and the sun protects your bones by producing "sunshine" vitamin D under your skin. Drinking and sunbathing are enjoyed by millions of people daily around the world. However, sunbathers have been informed how to sunbathe healthier and minimize the risk of sun damage. Drinkers have never been informed how they can drink healthier and minimize the risk of impaired immunity and alcohol-related organ damage until now!

You may have heard the expression, "On a hot day the sun really drains you." Basically, it means the sun drains your body of energy and water faster than you replace them. Notice I did not say faster than you "can" replace them, because you could replace both if you planned ahead to have a sports drink handy to drink periodically.

So how does the sun drain your body of energy and water? By making your body perspire. This water loss decreases the body's ability to extract energy from food, and muscle, which is mostly water, becomes dehydrated and weak. The dehydration, or loss of cellular water causes all cells, including muscle, to malfunction and you become fatigued. Dehydration and fatigue are treatable and preventable side effects of sun exposure. When you seek shelter from the sun the stress of the heat is removed. As you quench your thirst the cells refill with water and begin to function normally and your fatigue dissipates. Replacing fluids is the appropriate treatment for dehydration.

However, this treatment will not be enough to cure the dehydration and cellular malfunction caused by alcohol consumption. Unlike the sun, alcohol causes a massive urinary loss of vitamins, anti-oxidants, lipotropic factors, and minerals. Most drinkers neglect to replace these nutrients and the cellular malfunction will continue despite fluid replacement. In time, these cellular malfunctions will develop into alcohol-related health problems.

On hot sunny days your local newspaper and news stations provide you with a "burn index." This index approximates the number of minutes you can safely stay in the sun. Some even recommend which SPF (Sun Protective Factor) lotion should be used for that day, for example, SPF 2,4,6,8,15 or 30 lotion; the higher the number the greater the protection. The media reminds us there is a link between sun exposure and skin damage, and recommends minimizing our exposure between 10:00 a.m.-2:00 p.m. Health officials recommend the use of sunscreen, visors, hats, and sunglasses when outdoors.

Even if you never read a newspaper, magazine, or listened to a newscast about sun damage, it would be hard to miss the aisles of sunscreen displayed in every food and drug store. Suntan lotion is a billion dollar a year industry!

The label on sun lotion indicates that regular use helps reduce the chances of long term sun damage, such as premature aging, wrinkling, and skin cancer. All of this is very useful and practical information, a true public service that informs and enables us to minimize our risk. Even if we rarely spend time in the sun, we can pass the information on to our loved ones who do. Like dehydration and fatigue, skin damage is a preventable side effect of sun exposure.

In summary, sunbathing has known risks, such as premature aging, skin cancer, and general discomfort, if performed unprotected. Do we avoid the sun entirely based on these facts? No. Instead we sunbathe healthier by using protective sunscreens, wearing sunglasses and long clothes, and limiting exposure to the sun during its peak period. Moreover, we may use vitamin E lotion with lanolin and cocoa butter to replace moisture lost from the skin.

How come we know so much about sunbathing healthier? Someone informed us. Possibly our parents, family member, friend, or the media. Whatever the method, the information got to us and we chose to use it or ignore it. By following the do's and don'ts of sunbathing you can take more out of the sun than the sun takes out of you. Of course you may choose to ignore the rules of sunbathing healthier. However, when you develop wrinkles or skin cancer you should never say, "No one told me." Clearly, there was no lack of public information. If you willingly succumb to a preventable condition or disease, I must ask, "What color is the sky in your world?" I guess you can blame the suntan oil manufacturer and sue. After all, some dying smokers feel they have the right to sue big tobacco companies. Only in America!

If the idea of protecting your skin makes sense to you, drinking healthier will be equally appealing. Even if you do not drink, you can inform a loved one who does. Sunbathing healthier requires you to coat the outside surface of your body with a protective lotion. Drinking healthier requires you to coat your internal cells with protective life-force nutrients. There is no acceptable reason to willingly succumb to frequent illness, premature aging, hangovers, free radical and organ damage when there is a way to drink healthier.

Similar Risks Deserve Similar Treatments

From a health standpoint, sunbathing, prescription drug use, and drinking pose similar risks, and should receive similar treatment in terms of prevention. Alcohol is a drug, but it is not treated as such. You do not need a prescription to purchase alcohol. Therefore, you never receive alcohol-nutrient education at the time of purchase (do not be angry with the cashier; your doctor and pharmacist will not provide the education even if you mention that you drink heavily).

Prove it to yourself. Inform your local retail pharmacist that you consume five to seven drinks daily and have slight liver damage. You probably will receive a bewildered stare, and at best the pharmacist may tell you to reduce your consumption as he or she points you towards the alcohol section of the store. The pharmacist will not inform you to replace the life-force nutrients destroyed by alcohol or to use herbs. Why not? Because pharmacy school does not teach the pharmacist to view alcohol as a drug that has preventable side effects. To the pharmacist, dietitian, and physician, alcohol is a drug solely in terms of its intoxicating properties and potential for addiction. He does not view alcohol as a drug that requires a special program of life-force nutrient supplementation in order to prevent alcohol-related damage.

However, if you inform the same pharmacist that you are taking the tuberculosis medication Isoniazid, he will tell you to take supplemental vitamin B6. Why? Because he learned in pharmacy school that Isoniazid drains vitamin B6 from the body, and in order to maintain good health it needs to be replaced. Pharmacy school neglected to teach the pharmacist that the drug "alcohol" also drains the body of B-vitamins, minerals, lipotropic factors, and anti-oxidants. In order for the drinker to stay healthy these nutrients must be replaced and a program of herbal nutrition must be started.

If you are taking a prescription drug that causes a vitamin or mineral loss your doctor or pharmacist will advise you. If you choose to ignore the advice, you do so at your own peril. Drinkers have no guidance on how to drink healthier. No one is looking out for the drinker. The risk of drinking has not been minimized like the risks of sunbathing and prescription drug use, even though there are more year-round drinkers than year-round sunbathers and prescription drug users. The most startling fact of all is that the same drug stores that sell liquor and sunscreens also carry the life-force vitamins, minerals, anti-oxidants, lipotropic factors, and herbs required to drink healthier. The drinker with liquor in hand walks by an entire aisle of vitamins and herbs completely unaware that the answer to drinking healthier is right on the shelf. Once informed of the facts, I believe most drinkers would adopt the behavior of drinking healthier, just as most sunbathers and prescription drug users have adopted a healthier way to sunbathe and take medication respectively.

As a nation we are quite ignorant about the do's and don'ts of drinking. We know not to drive drunk or drink while pregnant, but we have yet to drink healthier as a way of minimizing alcohol-related health problems. This ignorance stems from the lack of public information on how to drink healthier. How come drinking does not receive the same treatment by the media as sunbathing? We never hear news stations saying, "If you will be drinking today, remember to take your life-force nutrients." How come we don't hear the surgeon general proclaim the need for vitamin, mineral, anti-oxidant, lipotropic factors, and herbal supplementation to minimize the ravages of drinking? Probably because no one wants to legitimize drinking in a health sense.

Drinking and becoming drunk stirs the deep pit of human emotion. Some people have been victimized by an individual under the influence of alcohol, or know someone who is a victim. The media and the medical community have chosen to keep an arm's distance from the fact that you can drink healthier. Has this been a good decision? No, because we are penalizing all drinkers, and their families, for the irresponsible actions of a small minority. Society expects a problem drinker to quit. Period. Society does not want a problem drinker to drink healthier, out of belief it will enable the drinker to drink more. This could not be further from the truth. Whether you're part of the small minority or majority, drinking healthier will simply reduce the odds of alcohol-related organ damage and impaired immunity as well as reducing the billions of dollars spent annually for treatment.

The health-care system has long denied the drinker access to health information while actively informing participants of other risky endeavors such as sunbathing, unsafe sex, needle sharing, and prescription drug use. This emotionally based decision to ignore the drinker is unfair to the millions of drinkers who would benefit from learning how to drink healthier. I believe if we can send convicted felons to prison, where they can work out with weights while they obtain their law degrees, we can provide a tax paying drinker with the opportunity to improve his or her own health.

As a registered nutritionist I am compelled to position drinking in an unemotional scientific light, a light that illuminates the fact that there is a way to drink healthier. I cannot influence the behavioral problems that a drinker may display. I leave that to the drinker and the behavioral therapy profession. Does that mean I should ignore what I can influence? Of course not. There is no excuse from a nutritional standpoint to deny the public access to information that can prevent illness, pain, organ dysfunction, and may even save a life.

Case Study

Ken was a 39-year-old attorney when he first sought my help. At that time he was going through a rather nasty divorce and admitted that his drinking had escalated. He would temporarily alleviate his severe depression each night with the help of six-to-eight scotch on the rocks.

Ken knew that drinking was not going to solve his problem, which was accepting the hard fact that his wife of eight years was having an affair with their landscaper. Over the year prior to coming to me, Ken usually consumed two to three drinks every night. His food intake was terrible in terms of providing his body with adequate vitamins and minerals. He last consumed vitamin supplements in the twelfth grade when he was a starting halfback. Ken complained of awful hangovers, chronic fatigue, bleeding gums when brushing, and tenderness in the calf area. Upon visual inspection, his tongue appeared smooth and dark red: a sign that he was deficient in riboflavin, folic acid and/or B-12. My immediate concern was Ken's declining health.

A three-day nutrient analysis supported my suspicion that Ken had classic vitamin and mineral deficiencies. Ken started my program of healthy drinking and within two weeks his symptoms were significantly lessened. One month later he visited again and his tongue was normal in appearance, and despite his continued drinking, Ken appeared to be a new man.

Two Theories on How Alcohol Damages the Liver

1. Alcohol has a direct damaging effect on the liver.
2. Alcohol has a direct damaging effect on the liver *only in the absence or insufficient presence of life-force nutrients.*

It is too easy to point a finger at alcohol and use it as a scapegoat rather than fully investigate all possible causes of liver damage. Why do some drinkers escape the pain and suffering of alcohol-related impairment of the immune system, liver, and pancreas, while others drink the same amount or less and fall victim? Clearly, there must be individual lifestyle choices in the area of nutrition and exercise that determine the outcome. Maybe we should be saying, "The drinker developed health problems after a lifelong habit of poor nutrition." This would be a more accurate assessment of the reason behind alcohol-related organ damage and impaired immunity. Genetics are also a factor; some individuals are genetically protected from developing complications despite a lifetime of heavy drinking.

A 1954 medical study mentions a gentleman who died at the age of 94 despite a sixty-year history of drinking a quart of scotch whisky daily. That is serious drinking. The drinker was a successful business owner, productive his entire life, who defied the odds and came out unscathed in terms of a debilitating disease. The study does not mention what type of nutrition plan the gentleman followed. However, I am guessing it was rather substantial, or he was riding on his genetics. Either way it flies in the face of theory number one.

Studies that support the first theory have used the baboon as an unwilling participant. One 1974 study fed thirteen baboons a so-called "nutritious" diet that was also very high in alcohol.

The amount of alcohol the baboons consumed was the equivalent of a 150-pound human drinking 40 ounces of 86 proof liquor per day. This daily consumption dwarfs the average alcoholic daily consumption. However, the researchers reasoned that because baboons have a faster metabolic rate they should be fed this level of alcohol. In my opinion this is nonsense. I bet they did not feed the poor baboons extra protective nutrients based on their higher metabolic rate.

Nonetheless, six baboons developed liver damage between nine months and four years from the start of the study. Even at this ridiculous daily level, less than half of the baboons developed liver disease. If they were fed the daily human alcoholic dose of 13-26 ounces of alcohol, and fed the complete range of life-force vitamins, anti-oxidants, lipotropic factors, minerals, and herbs, I would bet that outcome would have been very different. One must ask what they were really trying to prove in this study.

Other research shows that when alcohol was consumed with adequate nutrients it did not impair recovery from liver damage. This research does not support theory number one either. The problem with research used to support theory number one is the researchers never compare apples to apples; case in point is the baboon study. As a nutritionist, I support theory number two, which states that alcohol has a damaging effect on the liver only in the absence or insufficient presence of life-force nutrients. Until we see a properly constructed study that indicates a 21st Century Drinker can develop alcohol-related liver disease, theory number one has no basis for consideration. Theory number two makes sense and research supports the use of life-force nutrients. You can refer to the bibliography section of this book for complete references.

As for genetics, will we be so lucky as the 94-year-old gentleman who defied the odds? Maybe, maybe not. However, I do not believe in luck when it comes to drinking healthier; there is no luck involved, only skillful planning. Mind you, I believe in luck each time I play craps, cards, speed in the carpool lane when I have no passenger, and choose the checkout at the grocery store that has everyone paying with cash. I believe there is a special place in hell for anyone who waits until the cashier is finished totaling the bill, before they sign, date, and fill in the name of the store on the check. Clearly, this information should be completed upon arrival at the check-out. Then when the amount is determined it can be quickly entered. This is the only considerate method of check writing and should become law in all states. The 21st Century Drinker is trained to think and plan ahead, as this behavior is witnessed in drinking and check-writing skills!

The Path Food and Liquid Travel After You Swallow

Before we consider the path alcohol takes in the body, it is important that we understand the path food takes after we swallow. Imagine your 26 feet of gastrointestinal tract, that's right, 26 feet, which begins in the mouth and ends at your anus, as one long continuous recycling plant.

After you swallow, food and liquid travels down your throat into your stomach. Your stomach mixes the food with acid and digestive enzymes until it becomes the consistency of applesauce. If the food or liquid is contaminated the body ejects it by vomiting or producing a state of diarrhea. If the food and drink are safe the stomach slowly releases the mixture into the intestines at a rate of one ounce every few minutes. There the mixture is combined with more digestive enzymes and a fat-dis-solving liquid called bile, a liver "waste" product. The bile and enzymes separate the nutrients from the mixture, creating a nutrient "broth" that can now be absorbed into the body. The leftover mixture that was not absorbed is still the consistency of applesauce and travels into your large intestine, called the colon.

In the colon, water is absorbed from the applesauce-like mixture until it becomes firm. By now it has traveled beneath the lower left side of your belly button into an area called the rectal vault. Your body safely stores this material, now called "feces," until you get the urge to evacuate. At that point you voluntarily relax the strong anal sphincter and evacuate the entire length of your colon and sigh with gratifying relief.

To visualize this better, recall the last time you ate corn on the cob. You bit into the corn, chewed and then swallowed, you felt it pass down your throat and into your stomach. Your stomach churned the corn and released it into your small intestine where digestion and absorption took place. Some of the corn was broken down and absorbed, while the remainder passed into your colon. Upon evacuation you may have noticed that your stool was speckled with corn. If you did not notice, eat some corn and upon evacuation carefully peer into the bowl and study your specimen. You will note that some corn went completely through your recycling plant, and the nutrients in the corn were not separated out or absorbed. This is an example of malabsorption. Drinking causes malabsorption too, but in a different way.

Nonetheless, the result of drinking is lost nutrients and the beginnings of impaired health. I might add that the corn example is also referred to as the "reusable corn" theory, which states that in areas of the world where food is scarce, recycled corn may be a source of nutrition that could allow citizens to survive on the most meager food allowance. The kernels can be picked out, cleaned, dried, ground, and made into corn tortillas or related corn products. This is no joke. As a nutritionist, I studied the 1911-1917 period of the Mexican Revolution and was quite intrigued with the ingenuity of my southern neighbors in the use of corn kernels and other grains harvested from donkey dung!

While on the topic of evacuation I should mention that drinkers should have a larger than normal stool the morning after drinking. Passing a huge stool the moment you touch down on the toilet can be very gratifying compared to having your legs go numb as you sit and wait. Alcohol causes the stomach to produce excess acid, which combines with bile and pancreatic enzymes, causing a laxative effect that functions as an intestinal broom that sweeps the bowel clean.

Because alcohol causes dehydration, a drinker who consumes too little water can become constipated. A high-fiber diet can help this condition while swiftly expelling harmful bacteria from the body. Slow moving bowels create an opportunity for bacteria to attach to the intestinal wall and penetrate into the body. The medical term for this is bacterial translocation or "crossing over." Once the bacteria "cross over" inside the body they cause illness. Bacteria can also attack bile, converting it into potential cancer agents. Life-force nutrients "Teflon" coat the intestinal wall, preventing bacteria from sticking, and a high-fiber diet will bind and eliminate the toxic "creations" produced by bacteria.

Moreover, fiber increases stool girth which reduces your risk of diverticulosis, a common intestinal disorder caused by stools that are too small in diameter. A narrow stool forces the colon to squeeze down around the stool in order to push it forward.

The squeezing strains the colon causing little hernias or pockets to form in its lining. Food and bacteria become trapped in
the pockets causing the area to become infected, swollen,
painful, and can result in bloody, violent diarrhea. Therefore,
the passage of a good size stool is a healthful event not to be
missed or delayed.

The Path Alcohol Travels
After You Swallow

A champagne toast may symbolize recognition or honor. A
carefully set table, complete with wine glasses, may be the beginnings of a romantic intimate dinner for two. A frosty mug of
beer with a full head swelling over one side may signal the end
of the work day. An empty bottle of port wine in a brown paper bag may not have been enough. You can dress up alcohol
or you can dress it down. What alcohol represents to you may
vary from one drink to the next. However, to your body it
means one and only one thing: Work!

You may be in a bar and someone will buy you a drink. The
drink is a four-dollar savings to you, a four-dollar expenditure
or "investment" for whomever bought it, but physiologically it
will cost your liver plenty. The fact that you're celebrating,
mourning, or the drinks are free is of no consequence to the
liver. The liver does not peer out and say, "It's a free drink,"
or, "It's a wedding toast," and decide to process the load of
booze for free.

Normally, your recycling plant is tearing down the food and
liquids you consume by separating the nutrients from the
unusable material, absorbing the former, and discarding the
latter. The absorbed nutrients are shipped to the liver for distri-

bution to all areas of the body. Nutrients can be discarded by the recycling plant if the body has adequate supply and no room for additional storage. Alcohol has few nutrients to offer the body and requires no digestion. In the presence of alcohol the recycling plant and liver are disrupted. Alcohol speeds up the recycling plant and pushes the food nutrients through without being adequately absorbed. Alcohol also damages the delicate lining of the intestinal tract to the extent that vitamins and minerals are absorbed too little or too much.

The sum total of drinking in terms of nutrient balance is always negative, unless you follow the principles of drinking healthier and become a 21st Century Drinker. Alcohol's journey begins the moment it enters the mouth. So let us begin our journey. Let us look into the innards of a "recycling plant" where alcohol just arrived, shall we?

The tongue did not like the surprise. The 20,000 taste buds, usually a happy bunch, are revolting. Very few unpleasant items pass through the entrance of the recycling plant. Most are spit out and rejected, and rarely ever come close to the mouth again. Taste buds have a long memory and are responsible for keeping harmful food items out. Our sense of taste and smell protect us from eating harmful substances. There are three consumable categories that get past the taste buds without rejection. Each has received prior clearance from the brain, which controls all the actions of the recycling plant. The three categories are medicine, alcohol, and food cooked by someone you love who cannot cook well. The higher centers of the brain have reasoned that medicine and alcohol both initially taste bad, however, afterwards you feel exceedingly better. Therefore, the taste buds are forewarned by the brain never to reject these precious resources.

However, if you drink too much, or drink and eat the wrong foods, you will pay homage to the porcelain god. Over time the taste buds acquire a taste for alcohol, which is the only explanation for my penchant for Dewar's scotch, which I disliked intensely during our first meeting two decades ago. For the third category, the brain reasons that if the mouth spits out food prepared by a loved one, no matter how bad it tastes, other meals may not be forthcoming, and other organ systems may be penalized in turn! If you are painfully aware of this last situation, lead by example and demonstrate your culinary prowess; eat out, or just bear down.

A fast swallow sends the alcohol cascading down your throat like a waterfall, and it comes to an abrupt halt in the main holding area called the stomach. If you listen carefully you can hear the delicate tissue of your esophagus, known as the food pipe, whimper as the wetness of the alcohol stings each cell like salt in the eye. Smokers beware! Your risk of throat cancer and cancer in general rises dramatically due to alcohol's mutation of tobacco products — another strong reason to drink healthier.

In the stomach alcohol can go two ways. It can travel like a piece of food and proceed into the intestine or it can escape from the recycling plant by sneaking under the lining of the stomach and into the bloodstream. Whether alcohol stays in the stomach or sneaks out depends on how empty the stomach is, and how much alcohol dehydrogenase enzyme the stomach contains. Alcohol dehydrogenase destroys alcohol, preventing it from going in either direction; in a sense it neutralizes it. How much is neutralized depends on the amount, temperature, and type of alcohol beverage you drink and is discussed in Chapter 6. Men usually have more alcohol dehydrogenase than women, in addition to differences in body water and size. This helps explain why women tend to feel the effects of alcohol more quickly than men. However, as men age, the level of alcohol dehydrogenase activity declines to the level of women by the age of 50. This may explain why the tolerance of older male drinkers declines in their later years.

We shall first follow the alcohol that seeps quietly under the stomach lining and into the bloodstream. It seeps even faster on an empty stomach because there is no food blocking access to the lining. However, this does not mean drinking on a full stomach is a better choice.

Once in the blood, known as the body's highway, alcohol begins an all points destination trip throughout the body. Alcohol can travel to the brain in minutes. This direct route to the brain explains how alcohol quickly liberates us from inhibitions by sedating the reasoning center of the brain. All things become possible during this period of euphoria. We may reason that it's best to tell the boss off the next time he or she is a source of irritation.

However, we are more likely to use alcohol as a social lubricant or to feel carefree. If we drink faster than our ability to process alcohol, we begin to slur our speech, walk oddly, and eventually fall asleep or fall down. Either way we have lost the ability to interact socially. Alcohol is no longer a social lubricant; instead it is gumming up our ability to perform routine activities requiring simple coordination.

While in the brain, alcohol blocks the production of anti-diuretic hormone (ADH) which functions to keep water in the body. Because alcohol blocks ADH from retaining water, you find yourself frequently needing to urinate soon after you start drinking and long after you stop. You might be saying, "So what, it's just water weight, or just urine!" Indeed it is, but that water was removed from each cell in your body, including the brain. This cellular water loss causes the body to malfunction. Moreover, the urine is chock full of water soluble vitamins, anti-oxidants, and minerals that once belonged to the cells. These life-force nutrients are needed to properly process alcohol and must be replaced if you want to stay healthy. The losses affect the coordination of all muscles, including the heart, which depends on potassium and calcium for proper rhythmic beats. Similar dysfunction occurs in nerve tissue due to B-vitamin losses.

When your urine is coming out clear as spring water your body is in dire need of life-force nutrients. The processing of alcohol is being hindered along with every cellular process in your body. This means alcohol will circulate through the body longer creating additional cellular havoc. The damaged cells will leak out their nutrients, and the kidneys will excrete them as if they were excess supply.

After passing through the brain, alcohol travels once around the body unchanged. However, in order to go back up to the brain and around the body again it must pass through its "arch enemy," the liver. The liver is the main alcohol processing organ of the recycling plant. It filters the alcohol during each pass and hands it over to the "neutralizer" enzyme called alcohol dehydrogenase, located in the liver and partner of the stomach "neutralizer." Each pass through the liver weakens the alcohol dramatically, and if no other drinks are entering the mouth, the liver will clean up the alcohol at a rate of one to two drinks per hour. This work drains the liver of its cleaning supplies, which are B-complex vitamins, anti-oxidants, lipotropic factors, and minerals. Alcohol causes bile to clog the liver canals, and the best way to flush the liver out is by taking certain healing herbs.

The alcohol that does not sneak under the stomach lining is mixed with extra acid and empties into the intestines. The alcohol-acid mixture irritates the delicate lining of the intestines. Unlike the stomach, the intestines do not have a thick layer of mucus protecting the lining. The combination of alcohol, acid, and a short supply of life-force nutrients can cause ulcers to develop. In the intestines alcohol mingles with whatever happens to be present. Bile and enzymes are released but are not required to digest alcohol. The recycling plant is fooled into releasing its supplies, just like the kidneys were fooled into excreting precious nutrients. The alcohol is rapidly absorbed and sent to the liver for processing. Some of the alcohol will be neutralized, the rest will escape and race throughout the body to the brain. This process repeats until all the alcohol has been neutralized.

If you are a drinker who regularly imbibes you may activate a secondary processing plant in the liver called the microsomal ethanol oxidizing system (MEOS). The MEOS handles up to 40 percent of the alcohol load and explains why some drinkers have a higher tolerance for alcohol. No matter how the alcohol is processed, it is first converted into another "toxin" called acetaldehyde which in turn is converted to non-toxic acetate. Acetate can be burned as energy or used as a building block for many important substances.

When the last drop of alcohol has been processed, the brain, liver, stomach, pancreas, and intestines survey the damage in terms of lost supplies and need of cellular repair. If the life-force nutrients are delivered to these organs, they will heal and get ready for the next battle, and the drinker will enjoy years of better health while enjoying the pleasures of drinking. However, the organs know they are just workers in a recycling plant, and must use whatever nutrients are sent down by the drinker. If the food is low in nutrition, and life-force nutrients are nowhere to be found, battles will become harder to win, and the immune system and liver will falter. Then pain, illness and disease will raise their ugly heads and introduce themselves to the drinker through a series of attacks.

Case Study

Whenever I meet a drinker who appears well preserved despite his or her age, I perform a little detective work and begin a series of polite questioning. Clara was a delightful 89-year-old retired accountant whom I happened to meet while sitting at a bar in a Las Vegas casino. I noticed she had a penchant for vodka that was satisfied at a rate of two drinks every thirty minutes.

A little questioning revealed that she followed a drinking ritual that supported my own research. Clara never drank while eating. This decision was not based on anything other than the fact that she simply felt better afterwards. With each vodka she requested a glass of water. Instinctively, Clara knew alcohol caused dehydration. Her exact words were "I pee like nobody's business once I get started." Clara went on to tell me how she was raised on a farm and ate fresh produce daily. She still made her own fresh vegetable and fruit juices with the help of a juicer. Moreover, she regularly consumed various herbal teas and consumed a full range of vitamin and mineral supplements.

Clara started drinking during the height of prohibition when she was 17. Aside from some rheumatism, the only time she ever saw a doctor was when she went into labor with each of her five children. Interestingly, her son died at age 49 of a heart attack, and never had as much as a sip of beer his whole life!

Drinking Healthier Will Help to Prevent the Following Alcohol-Related Health Problems

- Nutrients in **bold** — Refer to Chapter 5 for how to take these nutrients
- Do not purchase individual minerals; buy a multi-mineral capsule
* Do not purchase these separately. These nutrients can be purchased as B-complex which allows you to take them all in one capsule.
** Nutrients can be found combined into one capsule.

Life-force Nutrients	How The Nutrient Is Lost During Drinking	Replenishing This Life-force Nutrient Will Help to Prevent:
Vitamin B1 (thiamin)* Frequently given to hospitalized drinkers to relieve mental and metabolic disorders. Nerves use sugar for energy. Without B1, sugar energy is not available for nerves, and the nerves cannot signal properly with muscle and other tissues.	Excreted in the urine	Inability to convert pyruvate, an end-product of sugar to energy. Instead, pyruvate is changed into lactate acid, resulting in lactacidosis — a lethal condition frequently encountered in alcoholics. This is the same acid that forms in exercising muscles causing a burning sensation; poor memory, enlarged heart, heart failure, abnormal heart beat, fatigue, impotence, nervous disorders, fatty liver, painful calf muscles, difficulty walking, mental confusion

Life-force Nutrients	How The Nutrient Is Lost During Drinking	Replenishing This Life-force Nutrient Will Help to Prevent:
Vitamin B2 (riboflavin)* Part of flavoproteins needed to properly process alcohol and food	Excreted in the urine	Fatigue due to poor release of energy from foods, red-puffy eyelids, sore tongue, cracks at the corners of the mouth, inability to activate niacin-based enzymes and carriers needed to process alcohol and acetaldehyde
Vitamin B3 (niacin)* Building block for enzymes and hydrogen carriers needed to process alcohol and acetaldehyde	Excreted in the urine	Mental confusion, lessened ability to process alcohol and food, fatigue, dermatitis, diarrhea, and unwanted weight loss
Vitamin B6 (pyridoxine)* B6 is needed to make lipoproteins that transport fat and cholesterol; lipotropic factors increase the burning of fatty acids. All the above help prevent a fatty liver.	Excreted in the urine; conversion of alcohol to acetaldehyde inactivates B6	Fatty liver, poor fatty acid metabolism, reduced level of lipotropic factors, nerve damage with numbness or pain in hands and feet, muscle weakness, inability to manufacture niacin, inability to form proteins or amino acids, lower immunity, hypoglycemia and dizziness due to inability to breakdown liver glycogen, poor liver repair
Vitamin B12 (cyanocobalamin)* B12 deficiency is often overlooked and not treated. Many drinkers exhibit mental changes despite having normal B12. Your doctor should test for homocysteine or methylmalonic acid levels to accurately identify a B12 deficiency.	Excreted in the bile and urine; poorly absorbed by alcohol damaged stomach lining or intestines; excessive use of antacids decreases B12 absorption; intestinal bacteria rob B12 from the body	Hallucinations, nervous disorders, numbness or pins and needles in hands and feet, paralysis, inability to form carnitine or DNA building blocks; throat, stomach, and intestinal ulcers due to reduced new cell growth; bleeding gums, painful beefy red tongue, pernicious and folate anemias, fatigue, inability to activate folate or reform methionine

Life-force Nutrients	How The Nutrient Is Lost During Drinking	Replenishing This Life-force Nutrient Will Help to Prevent:
Choline (lipotropic factor)* A component of lecithin and acetylcholine, a nerve transmitter involved in memory retention	Excreted in the urine along with B6, B12, and folate which are needed to self-manufacture choline; methionine may also be unavailable to form choline	Fatty liver, gallstones, cirrhosis, cholestasis (poor flow of bile), liver congestion
Folate (lipotropic factor)* Frequently given to hospitalized drinkers to relieve mental and metabolic disorders	Excreted in the urine	Inability to form the building blocks of DNA; anemia; poor wound healing; throat, stomach, and intestinal ulcers due to reduced new cell growth; bleeding gums; depression; mental confusion; inability to reform methionine
Biotin* Important co-factor in energy metabolism	Excreted in the urine	Depression; hallucinations; poor glycogen storage, muscle pain, weakness, scaly dermatitis, fatigue
Vitamin C (ascorbic acid) Anti-oxidant Activates white blood cells that protect against illness	Excreted in the urine	Infections; free radical damage; bleeding gums, poor wound healing; easily bruised skin; poor bile acid formation; formation of nitrosamines that may be linked to cancer; poor synthesis of adrenaline
Vitamin A and beta-carotene Anti-oxidant	Destroyed by liver microsomal ethanol oxidizing system (MEOS) which starts to process alcohol when high blood alcohol concentrations are reached; regular and binge drinkers can stimulate this method of processing (See *Chapter 5 for cautionary measures when taken by the heavy drinker.*)	Esophageal cancer: alcohol mutates tobacco products and increases your chances of cancer development; increased risk of upper respiratory infections because vitamin A is necessary for healthy mucus linings and cell development; night blindness; increased risk of infections

Life-force Nutrients	How The Nutrient Is Lost During Drinking	Replenishing This Life-force Nutrient Will Help to Prevent:
Vitamin D	Drinkers who rarely spend time outdoors do not self-manufacture vitamin D; known as the sunshine vitamin because the body produces it when your skin is exposed to the sun	Osteoporosis: vitamin D is required to absorb calcium from the recycling plant (intestines)
Vitamin E** Anti-oxidant; obese individuals require extra Vitamin E; high fat diets increase the need for vitamin E	Destroyed in the process of killing free radicals formed during alcohol processing; not absorbed if the drinker is selenium deficient	Free-radical damage to cell membranes and other lipid materials, liver disease, difficulty walking, calf muscle pain, red blood cell membrane destruction by free radicals, increased requirement for selenium when vitamin E is low
Vitamin K The overlooked "bone" vitamin	Antibiotics used to treat infections kill friendly bacteria in the intestines that make vitamin K; alcohol-damaged pancreas decreases absorption of vitamin K	Poor blood clotting, increased risk of hemorrhage, poor calcium retention by bone
Calcium (mineral) Helps build bone density. Not just for women! Male drinkers are at risk of developing osteoporosis in their later years	Excreted in the urine	Osteoporosis, abnormal blood clotting, blood pressure problems, muscle weakness, painful heel spurs, muscle spasms, cramps, twitching, shakes, sluggish bowel
Phosphorus (mineral) Part of ATP, a chemical that captures calorie energy from food and donates the energy to cells; given to hospitalized alcoholics to improve their condition	Excreted in the urine along with calcium; the following also deplete phosphorus: antacids containing aluminum and magnesium, diuretics, low dietary calcium	Fatigue, muscle weakness, difficulty walking or breathing, bone pain, hemolytic anemia, poor oxygen delivery to cells, impaired immunity, impaired DNA, poor development of cell membranes that require phospholipids, inability to activate methionine and other chemicals necessary for good health

Life-force Nutrients	How The Nutrient Is Lost During Drinking	Replenishing This Life-force Nutrient Will Help to Prevent:
Magnesium (mineral) Frequently given to hospitalized drinkers to relieve mental and metabolic disorders	Excreted in the urine; loss of magnesium causes increased loss of phosphorus	Poor protein formation, decreased cellular repair, high blood pressure, muscle twitches especially in the eye and face, confusion, fatigue
Zinc (mineral) Activates alcohol "neutralizing" enzymes; helps prevent acid build-up in blood	Excreted in the urine	Inefficient processing of alcohol and its by-product acetaldehyde, poor protein and DNA synthesis, poor wound healing and sperm production, testicular shrinkage, impotence, increased risk of infections, abnormal scar tissue formation, mental slowness, night blindness: zinc is needed to carry vitamin A to the eye, inability to convert lactate to pyruvate
Protein	Nitrogen, the building block of protein, is excreted in the urine; additional protein is required. *(Refer to Chapter 4 to determine your current intake and protein needs when drinking.)*	Lowered immunity and increased infections, poor cellular repair and liver regeneration, poor wound healing, fatty liver development
Water	Forced out from cells and changed to urine. *(Refer to Chapter 4 to determine your water needs when drinking.)*	Dehydration, mental confusion, poor digestion of food and incomplete energy metabolism
Selenium**(mineral) Anti-oxidant and part of the powerful free radical killer glutathione peroxidase	Destroyed by free radicals during the processing of alcohol and other liver "enemies"	Stiffening of the heart and liver tissues, fatty liver, cirrhosis, free radical and liver damage, poor digestion, reduced ability to buffer stomach acid

Life-force Nutrients	How The Nutrient Is Lost During Drinking	Replenishing This Life-force Nutrient Will Help to Prevent:
Potassium (mineral) Maintains normal fluid balance, muscle contraction and nerve impulses. Allows the stomach and intestines to push food along	Excreted in the urine or during vomiting. Diuretics also force potassium into the urine	Slow stomach emptying, slow bowels, muscle weakness, abnormal heart beat, high blood pressure
Chloride (mineral) Needed to make stomach acid (hydrochloric acid)	Excreted in the urine or during vomiting	Poor acidity of the stomach which results in poor protein digestion and B12 deficiency, poor iron and calcium absorption
Carnitine (lipotropic factor) Prevents fat build up in the liver	The B6 and B12 required to form carnitine are excreted in the urine; lack of methionine or lysine and/or damaged liver cells prevents the body from making its own carnitine	Fatty liver, inability to burn fat as an energy source, ascites or fluid-filled bloated abdomen
Cysteine (lipotropic factor) Required to make glutathione	Lack of B6 and methionine and/or damaged liver cells prevent the body making cysteine	Free radical damage and lowered ability to bind liver "enemies" and force them from the body
Methionine (amino acid and lipotropic factor) Required to make "binders" that excrete toxins from the body	Methionine is an essential amino acid that the body cannot make; quickly depleted during alcohol processing	Liver damage from free radical attack, inability to form cysteine or glutathione which are both needed to protect the liver; inability to make the correct DNA may lead to cancer development
Glutathione (tri-amino acid and lipotropic factor) Also an anti-oxidant, part of the powerful free radical killer glutathione peroxidase	Destroyed by acetaldehyde, free radicals, and alcohol induced oxidative stress; drinkers may not have the building blocks necessary to make glutathione	Fatty liver, fibrosis, cirrhosis, enlarged liver, free radical toxicity, ascites or fluid-filled bloated abdomen

Life-force Nutrients	How The Nutrient Is Lost During Drinking	Replenishing This Life-force Nutrient Will Help to Prevent:
Lecithin (lipotropic factor) Neutralizes acetaldehyde, the toxic byproduct of alcohol processing	The liver is unable to make lecithin when the building blocks — B6, B12, folate, and choline — are insufficient or there is existing liver damage	Fatty liver, fibrosis, cirrhosis, cell membrane changes that result in liver impairment due to phospholipid depletion, increased oxidative stress, ascites
Milk Thistle (herb) Liver cleanser and antioxidant, protector of liver function	Not found in the body	Poor flow of bile to the gallbladder, liver damage from free radical attack, poor protein synthesis and liver cell growth, cirrhosis, ascites
Dandelion (herb) Liver cleanser, helps detoxify	Not found in the body	Poor bile flow to the gallbladder and from the gallbladder to the intestines, gallstone formation
Artichokes (herb) Liver cleanser, helps detoxify	Not found in the body	Similar to the above
Goldenseal (herb) Blood purifier and immune booster	Not found in the body	Poor repair of damaged cells, lowered immunity and increased infections
Echinacea (herb) Natural antibiotic and immune booster, anti-infective, anti-inflammatory	Not found in the body	Frequent colds and infections, lowered immunity
Cayenne Pepper (herb) Vasodilator	Not found in the body	Poor circulation, poor healing of ulcers
Water soluble fiber Refer to Chapter 4 for food sources. Lowers cholesterol, traps liver "enemies" with its "sticky gum"	Not affected unless drinking replaces foods containing this type of fiber	Illness or infections from toxins re-entering the body after being sent out in the bile; high serum cholesterol

Clearly, alcohol can deplete the body of life-force nutrients. However, you have the power to control your fate and minimize the risks of drinking by learning to drink healthier. The first step is answering the question, *"What Type of Drinker Are You?"*

What Type of Drinker
Are You?

Too much bourbon is barely enough — Mark Twain

I have asked thousands of people the question, "What type of drinker are you?" The four most frequent responses are: (1) by the type of alcohol they drink — for example, a beer drinker, wine drinker, or scotch drinker; (2) by the amount of alcohol they typically consume — for example, a light drinker or heavy drinker; (3) by the behavior they exhibit during or after drinking — for example, a happy drinker or nasty drinker; (4) by how responsible they are, meaning they do not drive drunk or drink when pregnant.

When I probed further and asked them to describe their drinking abilities, they answered in terms of consumption rather than their ability to drink healthier or smarter. Never did they respond, "A drinker who drinks healthier." There was never a hint of understanding that they could learn to be savvier drinkers. This indicates that most drinkers view the activity of drinking on a superficial level. The thought process used in answering the question, "What type of drinker are you?" does not penetrate beyond the obvious, which is the act of drinking itself. However, when I asked, "What type of investor are you?" they may have said, "A stock, bond, commodity, or real estate investor." If I probed further they would describe their abilities as beginner, experienced, sophisticated, knowledgeable, prudent, successful, diversified, or "no money down" style of investing in real estate. Why didn't these drinkers view drinking in the same light as their investing?

It is frightening how nonchalantly drinkers blindly accept the risks of drinking, without attempting to ask, "Is there a safer or healthier way to drink that minimizes the known health risks of drinking?" Most drinkers would not blindly accept an investment opportunity without numerous questions on what the risks are and how they can be managed. It seems that they are more afraid of losing money than their health. Clearly both activities are risky and require their own special knowledge in order to be undertaken successfully.

There has been a shift in the drinking paradigm. The new set of rules teaches the drinker to view himself or herself as the controller over alcohol and not the controlled. Drinkers can now view drinking as they do other risky endeavors, and learn to reduce the risks through a risk management strategy called drinking healthier or how to become a 21st Century Drinker.

In 1988 I was a nutritionist at Community Hospital of Western Suffolk in Smithtown, New York. I had the opportunity to teach a twice weekly nutrition class to alcohol and substance abuse patients admitted into our twenty-eight day recovery program. Over the next nine years I refined my approach to improving the nutritional well-being of those who drank heavily. With the vision and common sense to realize that anyone who drinks alcohol could benefit from drinking healthier, I developed a friendly non-threatening way of describing how most people drink and how all can benefit from drinking healthier. I classify drinkers into eight categories which were developed during my interviews with the many drinkers I helped to drink healthier. Clearly, a person may be a hybrid of many drinking types during the course of a lifetime. The important point is all drinkers need to take life-force nutrients.

Before we go any further it is necessary to define a drink. Many drinkers may be surprised that a drink is defined by the amount of alcohol it contains and not the size of the glass. Each of the following is defined as one drink: 12-ounce beer, 4-5 ounce glass of wine, 10-ounce cooler, or 1.5-ounce of hard liquor. Therefore, if you grab a 16-ounce glass and add 3 ounces of rum over ice and fill the remainder of the glass with cola, you may think that is one drink, and in a way you're right. However, in terms of alcohol content, it is two! I have a friend who has only two drinks a day but they are made in an awfully large ceramic mug holding the alcohol equivalent of a six-pack of beer.

All Drinkers Can Benefit From Drinking Healthier

The Occasional Drinker: drinks at social occasions, weddings, funerals, parties, or other special events or nights out. He or she shies away from drinking as a means of heart protection due to the long-held belief that alcohol is bad for the health. Rarely does this person actually feel like drinking; it occurs mostly in response to being offered a drink or to feel at ease. This drinker usually requires help in determining what to drink since his drink vocabulary starts and ends with a "screwdriver."

Typical consumption is one to three drinks.

The Sports Fan Drinker: drinks at all of the above, and while cheering for a favorite team. Drinking can escalate depending how much the team is ahead or behind, and if a bet is being won or lost. This person likes to drink and often says, "Gotta beer?", "Wanna beer?", "Wanna shot?" He may or may not bring his own beverages to your house when invited to watch the big game. However, that's natural because free drinks always taste better. You may hear, "I lost count," or, "Who's counting?" when asking a Sports Fan how much he has drunk.

Typical consumption is four to eight drinks. Remember there is leeway here because some games end up going into overtime or provoke a greater than expected thirst. Moreover, he may not drink again until the next time his team plays.

The Weekend Drinker: drinks during the weekend and on social occasions, but really enjoys the effects of the booze and even has a favorite drink or two. He or she usually has a plan developed no later than Wednesday to drink on Friday and Saturday nights. Typically, this person is into the bar/club scene and is in search of Mr. or Ms. Right. At least a Mr. or Ms. Right for that night!

This is the toughest category to pinpoint consumption because most are using alcohol solely as a social lubricant. He or she may come into the bar relatively sober, scan the place and settle on an item of interest. Let the drinking begin!

For many Weekend Drinkers multiple "shots" of courage are par for the course. However, if the night is going slow in terms of mate potential, drinking is tapered and resources are saved for another night that may hold greater promise. Some Weekend Drinkers, in an effort to save money, will have a few drinks at home, and one "parking lot" drink before proceeding into the bar. This may be a lingering trait from earlier years spent in the college drinking mode.

Typical consumption is two to eight drinks.

The College Drinker: drinks at all of the above. The cost of the alcohol always prevails over the quality. She drinks as much as she can prior to arriving at the party or bar and attempts to consume as many free drinks as humanly possible. She often states something about the "marginal utility" of each drink, a concept she is validating for an Economics 101 class. The College Drinker has no limits and she usually has no job to wake up for in the morning. And no self-respecting College Drinker regularly attends an 8:00 a.m. class. Vomiting seems to be essential and may even be a prerequisite.

Body shots are common. The number one liquor used for a body shot is tequila. Other ingredients needed are salt, lime, and a very close friend who does not mind you licking a part of her body. Basically, the drinker licks or "limes" up the body spot of choice, salts the wetness to taste, then licks that spot clean after swallowing the shot of tequila. To show enthusiasm, the drinker can lick it before and after. (Body shots beat licking your own hand if you have the right partner.) College Drinkers who practice this art form never develop a vitamin C deficiency because limes and lemons are recommended sources of vitamin

C. However, if they stop indulging in body shots their immune system suffers. The wonders of vitamin C and youth!

Typical consumption is "too much is barely enough" for this group.

Case Study

During my seminar, "Good Nutrition and How It Can Combat Stress," I mentioned various aspects of healthy drinking. At the end of the seminar a woman approached me and asked if she could make an appointment for her son who was starting college in two weeks. She was concerned about campus binge drinking and wanted to prepare her son for the inevitable. She knew he already attended local keg parties and she allowed him to drink moderately at home.

Steve was 18 when we first met. I knew immediately this was an opportunity to make a life-long impact. Steve was captain of his football team, lifted weights, and appeared to be headed for success. We met privately and Steve proceeded to tell me the extent of his drinking. I would describe his drinking as competitive tournament-style drinking. Drinking contests were regular occurrences in Steve's circle of friends. Undoubtedly, this behavior would continue into his freshman year. Steve experienced brutal hangovers, but he had the entire next day to recuperate because he did not have a job. However, with a full load of classes he could not afford to be hung over when school started.

I educated Steve that drinking was serious business, and if he was going to drink he must learn to drink healthier. Steve followed my instructions, and even told me he was charging his fraternity brothers for access to his secrets of healthier drinking! Over time, Steve developed a greater respect for alcohol and rarely consumed alcohol unprotected.

The Regular Drinker: drinks at all of the above, on a regular basis, or daily. Even if he didn't go to college, he probably drank like a college student during some point in his life. I remember an advertisement that read, "Be a model or just look like one." You may not have gone to college, but at some point in time you probably drank like the College

Drinker. It's an American and almost universal rite of passage into adulthood. After all, adulthood is the starting line where the real fun begins.

It is important not to prejudge the Regular Drinker because many are trying to achieve the full benefit of alcohol's cardiovascular protective benefits. This person likes to drink and has numerous favorite drinks, but one or two mainstays. He also has a great deal of faith in alcohol's therapeutic properties and may slightly increase consumption for medicinal purposes. A good drink after a hard day of negotiating helps this drinker's transition from work time to quality time. I use "negotiating" as a catch-all term for whatever the drinker had to do in order to get through the day in one piece.

Typical daily consumption is two to ten drinks. Bettors beware! Regular Drinkers can hold their own against any Sports Fan, with the exception of a Raider fan during a Super Bowl in which the Raiders are behind 27-21 with one minute left in the fourth and are threatening inside the opponents' 20-yard line.

The Executive Drinker: attends countless business lunches, dinners, and seminar or convention-type meetings. She frequently entertains clients who expect to be wined and dined. This expectation requires the Executive Drinker to be very flexible in terms of eating and drinking. In fact she may end up eating and drinking just to make the client feel comfortable. Three martini lunches are making a business comeback. Cigars and hard liquor are once again in vogue, as is a confident attitude that drinking can round out a meal when working on a deal. When negotiating terms, the confident Executive Drinker orders drinks even if her client appears to be a non-drinker. If the deal is right the client will not terminate the deal unless she vomits on the contract or makes unsolicited and unwanted sexual advances.

Typical consumption is four to eight drinks, although, the stress and celebration that comes with doing business can cause the consumption of food and drink to escalate.

Case Study

Carl, 47 and his wife Toni, 41 owned a marketing consulting business. They often wined and dined prospective clients, but the frequency was beginning to take its toll. They approached me after a wellness seminar and requested an appointment to help determine how they could drink healthier. They both had put on 15 pounds over the last year and blamed alcohol as the culprit.

They felt they received more business when they indulged with a prospective client. Drinking seemed to relax all involved, and business negotiations went much smoother to the benefit of all parties. Therefore, they were quite excited when they heard me mention that alcohol is not responsible for weight gain. Carl and Toni learned that the food choices they made before, during, and after drinking directly contributed to their weight gain. By simply following the information on which foods to consume and avoid before, during, and after drinking, they each lost approximately 15 pounds within three months.

The Alcoholic Drinker: clearly, an alcoholic can be found in the any of the above categories. There is no typical alcoholic. Alcoholics are not weak, lazy or incompetent, (although some are, just like some tea drinkers are). Not all alcoholics miss work, beat their kids or significant other. They don't all drink and drive. Drunk driving accidents are due to drunk drivers, and the drunk driver is not always an alcoholic.

I know many alcoholics who are successful business people and only drink after work and on their days off. They would never drink on the job and jeopardize their careers. They have learned to postpone their drinking to the appropriate time.

When the work day is done the drinking begins and may continue until they pass out. This is their daily routine and they cannot stop. In fact they don't want to stop.

Case Study

Jim was a 57-year-old construction foreman and an alcoholic who drank daily — heavily — for the past 40 years. Ten years earlier his doctor noticed that Jim's blood work indicated liver trouble. His doctor inquired how much alcohol Jim consumed. Naturally, Jim said he was a social drinker and the doctor did not press further. As the years went by Jim developed health problems such as limb numbness, mental confusion, and full-blown liver attacks.

Finally, Jim informed his doctor about his true nightly consumption of ten shots of whiskey, or five shots and five beers nightly. Jim's doctor informed him that continued drinking would surely kill him. His advice was something Jim would never follow. The advice was to quit drinking. Jim came to see me after a drinking buddy who attended my nutrition class told him there was an alternative. I was deeply frustrated when Jim relayed his story concerning his doctor's advice. I told Jim that my program was the best chance he had to live a longer life. I agreed with his doctor, Jim was on a path of self-destruction. However, I chose to alter Jim's path. I took the time to do a complete nutrient analysis that revealed that Jim was deficient in almost all nutrients. I then provided Jim with a healthier drinking plan. Months later Jim told me that at his recent physical, the doctor thought Jim had curtailed his drinking because his blood work improved! Jim did not let on that he was still drinking as much as ever.

My reason for writing this book is not to describe what an alcoholic is or how to treat the alcoholic in order to achieve abstinence. That is not my professional area. I wrote this book to teach everyone who drinks that there is a way to drink healthier. Until an alcoholic is ready to stop drinking he or she should be informed how to use vitamins, lipotropic factors, anti-oxidants, herbs, protein, and minerals in order to protect the liver and overall health. I offer this education to anyone who drinks, especially the heavy drinker. Good nutrition can extend the life of any drinker and the fact that this has not been addressed by the medical community is a real travesty.

Typical consumption can range from 13 to 32 ounces of hard liquor a day, or the wine or beer equivalent.

The 21ˢᵗ Century Drinker: rare individuals who invested time into learning how to drink healthier. They have taken responsibility for their decision to drink by taking the time to prepare their bodies for meeting with alcohol. They feel better and healthier than drinkers who do not know how to drink healthier. They have a plan to minimize the health consequences of drinking. They may never have more than one or two drinks, or they may drink like a fish.

In the hands of a 21ˢᵗ Century Drinker, alcohol is a multipurpose tool that can be healthfully applied to a number of life's inevitable moments such as the desire to celebrate, unwind, mourn, contemplate, seek inner clarity, sort thoughts and emotions, socialize, and feel a temporary confidence needed to take a first step. None of the above equates to using alcohol as a crutch as many people would have you believe. It is normal behavior, plain and simple.

Typical consumption is enough to achieve their definition of a balanced productive life. Consumption has been known to decrease as the 21ˢᵗ Century Drinker learns to find balance through Cycle Drinking as discussed in the next chapter.

No matter what type of drinker you are today you need to start drinking healthier like the 21ˢᵗ Century Drinker. The average person is eating on the run and skipping meals in an effort to lose weight. This person cannot efficiently process alcohol at even the lowest level of consumption. Even if he or she drinks only two drinks, the body is being drained of life-force nutrients and a mediocre diet is not adequately replacing them.

I am a 21st Century Drinker. This means I know how to drink healthier and have minimized the chances of developing alcohol-related health problems. I have enjoyed drinking during the last twenty years. I plan to be able to continue this enjoyment well into the 21st century or until the good Lord takes me. I have great memories of fun times shared with friends and family, from wedding toasts to funerals and backyard barbecues. Drinking was a way to celebrate, mourn, and at times enabled me to tolerate certain social gatherings. God bless the availability of the grape when all you are hearing from someone is yada, yada, yada.

Well, maybe the occasions weren't all fun, but it sure made the tough times not so tough and I always strive for balance, which is key. If I was asked *before* I started to drink healthier if I ever abused alcohol I would have said, "You bet, and with a passion." However, I never physically or verbally abused my girlfriend, or anyone or anything during my dance with the bottle. Drinking never interfered with my ability to hold a job or earn two Master degrees. Alcohol was something that felt good like money in my pocket, a song in my heart, or a pretty woman on my arm.

So why not indulge? Life is too short, but it's even shorter for drinkers who do not take the time to drink healthier.

If I was asked *today* if I ever abused alcohol before I started drinking healthier I would say, "Hell no, it was abusing me by draining my life-force nutrients and leaving me high and dry." Pun intended. It's just that I view drinking in a scientific light today. I feel the same about alcohol as I did back then. I still like the way alcohol affects me. I still like the way wine and liquor bottles look when they are lined up neatly on a shelf. I still love going to wineries and sampling all the free wine I can accommodate. Hell, that's one of the reasons why I moved to California! The fragrance of wine is still invigorating and the taste is delightfully superb. I still love the sound of ice clinking gently into my favorite glass, and the popping sound the ice makes as the liquor kisses it for the first time. I still like the eye appeal of a well dressed drink complete with a rim garnish when appropriate, and always with a real stirrer and bar napkin.

I drink whenever I want, which can be sporadic or daily, almost daily or not for two weeks. I have a range of two to ten drinks per session, and no, I am not an alcoholic. I thank God and the vitamin and herbal industry that my health is good after twenty years of steady imbibing.

I ask you now, "What type of drinker do you want to be?" If you answered a 21st Century Drinker, turn the page and start your journey on the road to wellness!

How to Become a 21st Century Drinker

It is not abstinence from pleasures that is best, but mastery over them without being worsted — Aristippus

It is important that there is no misunderstanding about the purpose of ***Drink as Much as You Want and Live Longer*** or the definition of a 21st Century Drinker. When I started writing this book people would bring up the subject of alcoholism and the alcoholic. They would say an alcoholic could not drink healthier and the only safe solution is to quit drinking. In turn I would ask, "How do you define healthier?"

Their response was always a litany of mental health descriptions such as normal behavior, good judgment, being responsible, and the like. That is not what I mean by healthier.

I am a nutritionist viewing drinking from a nutritional perspective. I can teach you to drink healthier in terms of protecting your immune system and internal organs, healthier in terms of reducing the risk of an overweight belly, hangover, liver disease, and other alcohol-related health problems. I am not suggesting that an alcoholic who has been dry can read this book and suddenly have control over alcohol through the use of life-force nutrients. If drinking caused you to lose control of your life you probably should not drink. However, none of that has anything to do with the fact that anyone, including the practicing alcoholic, can drink healthier.

Principles of 21st Century Drinking

It is important to list the principles of 21st Century Drinking at this time to enable you to develop the philosophy of a 21st Century Drinker. Some of the principles below have been discussed in previous chapters and others will be discussed throughout the remainder of the book.

- Drinking will age you, drinking healthier will not
- Drinking weakens your body, drinking healthier returns your strength
- Drink healthier for yourself or someone else, but do it and do it consistently
- Always assess how the next drink will affect you — determine the marginal utility

- Physical well-being should never be allowed to erode during the use of alcohol
- We all must die one day, but not from liver failure
- Forget the dog, the drinker's best friend is the liver!
- Life-force nutrients are the required premium for all drinkers
- Never buy premium booze if it means skimping on life-force nutrients
- The liver lacks taste buds, but hungers for life-force nutrients
- Always urinate a deep rich yellow
- Always evacuate the colon the morning after drinking
- Drinking opportunities will always come up so have your body prepared
- Invest in a pocket-size pill box and never leave home without it

Philosophy of the 21st Century Drinker

Like many of you I have grown weary of the ever growing list of no-nos.

No fried or fatty foods, no salty or sugary snacks, no cigar smoking, no drinking, and the like. Enough is enough. There is a healthy approach to drinking which will enable you to enjoy one of life's simple low-tech pleasures. The 21st Century Drinker is not afraid of alcohol, and certainly would not just say no to it like a mindless idiot who needs the government to make all of life's tough calls.

The 21st Century Drinkers are people who know how to drink healthier. They know that the risk of alcohol-related health problems increases with decreasing life-force nutrient stores. Throughout a lifetime of drinking, the 21st Century Drinkers beat the odds of incurring alcohol-related health problems, premature aging, and frequent illness. They beat the odds because they understand the factors that make up the odds and they have a plan. These are no ordinary individuals, but were once no different than you.

The voice of reason shouts, "If you have already decided to drink, you must learn to be a 21st Century Drinker and protect your health." Anything less is pure foolishness. Your health is too important to leave it up to chance. Do you want to know how you can drink healthier? If you answered yes, congratulations! You have just taken a giant step towards improving your own health and the health of a loved one who drinks. It all comes down to having a plan and respect for alcohol.

By respecting alcohol you have respect for yourself. When you have respect for yourself, you are half way to where you want to go.

The Amateur Drinker

I do not judge why someone drinks. Neither should you. I leave that to the drinker, and the many critics who so readily pass unwanted judgment. Although there are many good reasons to drink, there is no good reason to drink like an amateur. I was once an Amateur Drinker, although at the time I thought I was a fairly respectable semi-pro drinker. I would challenge my liver with an assortment of nightly indulgences ranging from a dozen shots of low grade tequila, to a bottle of wine and a tall cold King Cobra malt liquor. Johnny Walker and his cousin Jim Beam were regular guests in my home when Jack Daniels was unavailable.

During my teens and twenties youth was on my side and my recuperative abilities were strong. However, now I no longer rely on the recuperative powers of youth. Instead I drink healthier. I am the original 21st Century Drinker. Youth deceives you into believing that no damage can occur. But I have known people, including family members, who have experienced the ravages of what I now call complications of amateur drinking.

They did not know anything about preventive care through nutritional supplements. You probably know someone who has developed an alcohol-related health problem, too. Would you describe that individual as someone who followed a nutritional plan that replaced the protein and life-force nutrients lost during alcohol metabolism? Did he periodically use herbs to detoxify his liver? Probably not, and that's the main reason he became ill.

Being an Amateur Drinker has nothing to do with the ability to drink. It is the inability to prepare the body for the drinking bout. I call it a bout because it's very much like a boxing bout except your opponent is alcohol. Each shot of liquor, sip of wine, or guzzle of beer is an unprotected body blow. Amateur Drinkers will always lose their health to alcohol because they lack a fight plan. No self-respecting fighter accepts a bout and then shows up unprepared. Months before the bout the fighter begins supplementing his diet, training relentlessly on the heavy bag, speed bag, and with a number of sparring partners. The fighter has planned running, jumping rope, and weight-lifting sessions. For each of the twelve rounds of fighting there is an established fight plan and contingency plan. Nothing is left to chance. The night before the fight, the fighter gets a good night's sleep. In the morning and again in the early afternoon, the fighter consumes energy rich carbohydrates to fuel his muscles during the fight.

Finally, the time is at hand to do battle. The fighter carefully wraps his hands and puts on protective gloves. Then and only then does the fighter step into the ring, face his opponent, and exchange numerous body and head blows. Between rounds the fighter rests, drinks water, regroups, and focuses on the battle to come in the next round. The carbohydrate energy stored in the muscles of the arms and legs allows the fighter to keep on fighting with power. In the end the fighter emerges victorious having out-smarted and out-powered his opponent through strategic planning and the desire to fight forever.

Fortunately for the fighter, the entire fight can last a maximum of thirty-six minutes. A drinking bout can last hours or a lifetime. Each drink translates into an unprotected blow that weakens the body, and if repeated frequently, the body succumbs to illness. Unlike the fighter, alcohol doesn't wear gloves and can sneak up on the drinker. However, no pain is felt during the drinking bout. The only similarity between the fighter and the amateur drinker is they both feel pain the morning after their bouts, and until recently only the drinker was at risk of being on the receiving end of a "bite." However, after the 1997 Holyfield-Tyson fight this no longer holds true. The drinker's "bite" is a figurative term for "cheap alcohol" or "strong alcohol" that feels harsh going down. The boxer's "bite" literally means a "bite" out of the ear. Luckily, the drinker's "bite" rarely requires medical attention, and future incidences can be kept to a minimum by upgrading to a brand name.

Amateur Drinkers do not plan to have failing health. They fail to plan for good health. The Amateur Drinker makes no preparations for an upcoming drinking bout. In fact, she may have finished a drinking bout within the last twenty-four hours. The morning of her next bout she skips breakfast and possibly grabs a doughnut and coffee later that morning. The headache and dry mouth are subtle reminders of the night before. The amateur drinker attributes the hangover to the realities of drinking and not to a lack of planning. However, not knowing any better, the Amateur Drinker tries to remedy her thirst by drinking more coffee, cola, or whatever beverage is available. Whereas, the boxer knows the importance of "carbohydrate loading" to ensure the muscles have fuel during the fight, the Amateur Drinker does not know the importance of "fueling" up the liver with life-force nutrients before, during, and after drinking. The Amateur Drinker's food and beverage choices prove this.

Meanwhile, inside the drinker's body, the liver is frantically straining the blood in search of life-force nutrients to repair the damage from the previous drinking bout. If the liver had a head it would shake it gravely at the incoming blood laden with caffeine, sugar, and fat. If it had a voice it would bellow, "Where is my protein? Where are the life-force nutrient replacements? Don't you know I fought a battle here last night? How do you expect me to keep you healthy? My filter is clogged with waste and toxins; send down the herbal cleansers. Send me reinforcements before the enemy comes again or I will be forced to curtail activity at the expense of the entire organism. Please refrain from eating so much fat; it's clogging me up."

Unfortunately, the liver has no voice to warn the Amateur Drinker. At lunch time the Amateur Drinker eats whatever looks good to the eyes, taste buds, wallet or purse. The food chosen is based on the Amateur Drinker's psychological need to eat. No thought is given to the physiological needs of the liver or the body. It's as if the Amateur Drinker is unaware that the liver requires special nutrition when alcohol is consumed.

At the end of the workday the Amateur Drinker decides to have a rematch with alcohol. Each drink consumed becomes another unprotected body blow affecting all systems, especially the immune, liver, stomach, intestines, brain, and pancreas. Between rounds, if the bout is taking place in a bar, the drinker inhales second hand smoke, munches beer nuts, makes idle banter, and goes to the restroom to urinate "cell water" full of life-force vitamins, anti-oxidants, and minerals desperately needed by the liver. In the end, alcohol emerges victorious once again, and a little more life is drained from the amateur drinker.

Then one day after years of unprotected body blows, the liver or one of the other systems damaged by alcohol causes the Amateur Drinker to scream out in pain. Drinking is always a losing proposition for the Amateur Drinker. The scenario repeats until the Amateur Drinker tires of being weakened by alcohol and chooses to become a 21st Century Drinker. A smart choice considering the alternative: poor quality of life and a slow agonizing demise.

Learning to Plan

Just as a fighter must prepare for his bout, you must prepare your body for its bout with alcohol. Believe me when I say alcohol is a stern and unforgiving competitor, and must be taken seriously. You must show some respect. You should not just at the spur of the moment say, " Give me a double vodka," without having prepared your body. Why subject your body to unprotected body blows? It's a losing proposition which only weakens you into making other losing propositions. You must learn to protect your body against alcohol just as the fighter protects himself against his adversary. Don't worry, I have no intention of having you skip rope, run ten miles a day, spar for months, or drink raw eggs. However, my intentions are equally beneficial. I plan to change your behavior and change the very way you go about your drinking. I am going to add a few steps to your drinking ritual. I am going to raise your drinking to an art form. You will become a 21st Century Drinker.

All successful businesses and business people use a plan to guide them along the road to financial success. Likewise, 21st Century Drinking requires that you follow a nutritional plan with a special focus on prevention of alcohol-related illness and immune dysfunction. Drinking healthier has probably never been a focused goal for most people who drink. The goal of many drinkers is to quench a thirst and get a little drunk, an admirable goal especially in today's demanding world of goal setting. At least satisfying a thirst and achieving a world-class buzz are obtainable short-term goals unless you run out of booze. Therefore, the "just in time" method of inventory management should never be applied to your bar stock.

If you're going to drink or get drunk, you must drink like a 21st Century Drinker. It begins with knowing a little about alcohol. Alcohol is a guest who demands specific accommodations. How well you prepare for the arrival of alcohol determines how happy the visit will turn out for you. Alcohol is like someone who brings happiness in one hand, and like a bandit, uses the other to rob your body of life-force vitamins, minerals, anti-oxidants, lipotropic factors, protein, and cellular water.

Twenty-First Century drinking requires that you plan your drinking with the same dedication as your retirement or annual vacation. The goal of a 21st Century Drinker is to maintain good health throughout a lifetime of drinking. This goal is achieved by planning, planning, and more planning.

If you are saving for retirement you have a plan that will enable you to retire someday with financial security. This is good. You have demonstrated the ability to plan for your future needs. If your retirement is invested in the stock market you probably have diversified your portfolio to minimize market risk. This is good also. You have demonstrated the ability to recognize that with investment there is risk, and instead of avoiding the stock market you choose to minimize the risk through diversification.

Developing the ability to plan and minimize risk in the long and short run are attributes of a good investor. If you can plan for retirement you can and should develop the ability to be a 21st Century Drinker. After all, you can be planning for a picture-perfect retirement, but if you arrive at retirement age weakened by alcohol-related health problems the picture certainly will dim. The investor saving for retirement primarily focuses on the future; the 21st Century Drinker must focus on the present. Each drinking bout presents a short and long-term risk which can be minimized by practicing the three steps of drinking healthier discussed in Chapter 5. The 21st Century Drinker knows that drinking is a risky venture; however, by using life-force nutrients the drinker minimizes the risk and achieves peace of mind.

Each time a 21st Century Drinker drinks he poses the following question: "If my body/liver were a publicly traded company would investors be buying shares in my company? Or would they be selling them? Or God forbid selling them short!" Selling short means that investors who do not own stock in your company are borrowing the shares and immediately selling them. They believe that problems are festering in your company and the shares will soon decrease in price. Therefore, they sell the overvalued borrowed shares, and buy them back after they fall in value. The difference between the selling and buying price is their profit. If your drinking causes investors to sell their investment in you, or prevents them from making an initial investment, drinking healthier can reverse that sentiment.

When a company wants to reverse negative investor sentiment the company president writes a letter to the shareholders. The letter details the positive changes occurring in the company and any future developments. This message is typically the first page of the company annual report. A drinker who converts to 21st Century Drinking could write a similar letter to inform and attract investors.

Remember, your shareholders are the people who have a stake in your future. Your family, friends, business partners, and employer will not hesitate to invest in you if the risk reward ratio is favorable. Planning with an eye on the present, and treating the act of drinking as a business activity is all it takes to ensure your retirement years are pretty as a picture.

Dear Shareholders:

The decade-long drain on my physical capital has come to an end.

No, I have not stopped drinking, but during the last quarter I have started drinking healthier. The likelihood of this body remaining productive has never been brighter since conception.

The new risk-management program *Drink as Much as You Want and Live Longer* was procured and implemented with a minimal outlay of capital. Moreover, the return on investment substantially exceeds that required by our company. However, the lifelong plan of ingesting life-force nutrients will require an ongoing commitment of working capital.

This extra capital will be made available from the expected increases in productivity which will translate into increased earned income. However, during times of restricted cash flow, management will switch to a lower cost beverage to ensure that life-force nutrients are always available.

A secondary stock offering is being planned next quarter due to recent investor interest and an upgrade of all my outstanding debts by all major rating services. This is testimony that the recent decision to start drinking healthier has removed the dark clouds that once surrounded my body.

I am certain the future will be full of opportunities, and my body is poised to take advantage of those that will increase shareholder value.

Thank you for your past and continued support. I look forward to seeing all of you at the annual shareholders meeting.

Sincerely,

President and 21st Century Drinker
My Body/Liver, INC.

Case Study

The realization that you will not live long enough to enjoy the fruits of your labor can be quite sobering. Bob planned for the good life. As a company president, Bob commanded a $250,000 salary before bonus and stock options. He could tell you all about his 401k and mutual fund plans. He was a walking prospectus on just about any major mutual fund. He even earmarked future bonuses to this plan or that one. No detail was overlooked in his quest for financial independence and the security of a well-financed retirement. The only thing Bob overlooked was the one thing money could not buy, and that was good health.

Bob was 50 years old, 5'8" and weighed a sloppy 210 pounds. He enjoyed great quantities of cognac and wine daily. Hard liquor and beer were no strangers to his palate either. With chicken legs and a belly that rivaled that of a pregnant woman, Bob was a sight to see lounging around the pool reading the *Wall Street Journal.* I was on vacation in Tucson, Arizona, when I met Bob at the hotel where I was staying. I asked if I could read the finance section of his paper and he obliged. My repeated ordering of scotch and water from the pool waitress peaked Bob's interest and he asked how I could drink so much and be so fit. I explained to Bob a little about my program, and then began to depart. At that moment, Bob asked if he could consult with me. I explained that my office was in New York, but Bob was insistent that I give him my number for he traveled to New York frequently. I gave Bob my number and never thought of him until two months later when he called to say he would be in my area the next week!

Bob had recently lost a very good friend who died from liver failure. He died a miserable death, hooked to every imaginable tube, and treated without pity as if his dying was tough luck. His friend did not receive the compassion reserved for a cancer patient or victim of an assault. This deeply concerned Bob. He was willing to pay almost any price for life extension, or at the very least a better shot at living a longer life. Clearly, Bob had much to lose. In addition to his wealth he had a beautiful wife and three college-age children. Bob was motivated to follow my program because he could see the payoff — he did not have to quit drinking in order to see his retirement plans come true. Over the next year, Bob lost thirty-five pounds and was consuming enough life-force nutrients to minimize liver damage. He believes he was saved from the fate his friend met all too soon. So do I.

Cycle Drinking: The Only Way to Rest Your Liver and Still Drink

Cycle Drinking is not self-deprivation, it is self-preservation. The idea behind Cycle Drinking is balancing the need to drink with the liver's need to rest. The liver is a tough character and can tolerate a great deal of neglect. It is not a whiner like the stomach, muscles, eyes, ears, rectum, teeth, gums, or throat. You never feel pain in your liver until it is really sick. An organ like the liver should be respected and protected like the family jewels.

I am sure you work hard at your job and expect to receive a couple of days off each week to recuperate. Moreover, you probably receive sick days and two weeks paid time off for vacation. In comparison, the liver is never allowed to rest until you die; however, it does appreciate a lower work load now and then. A 21st Century Drinker views Cycle Drinking as a workout for the liver that has varying levels of intensity so it doesn't burn out. This is a simple principle to understand but difficult for amateur drinkers to put into practice.

The concept of cycle training in weight lifting is well known. A weight lifter does not train the biceps everyday because the biceps would become weaker and smaller due to overtraining. Moreover, the same type of curling motion is not repeated workout after workout. The weight lifter chooses slightly different motions to stimulate the biceps and varies the number of repetitions and sets performed. A weight lifter does not go to the gym each night and attempt to squat or bench press his or her maximum. Why not? Because the muscle tissue would whine, and the weight lifter realizes that muscle tissue cannot repair overnight. Even weight lifters who love bench pressing control their zeal for pectoral training to once or twice a week.

Because muscles can ache and are visible, it is easy to assess if you are overtraining them. The same cannot be said for the liver.

You probably have never assessed your liver. In fact most people do not even know where it resides. The liver is hidden under the lower right half of your rib cage. This makes it problematic in terms of viewing. Out of sight, out of mind equates to neglect when it comes to the liver. When your liver is damaged it becomes swollen and discolored, and it may have fatty streaks. However, the damage is so silent that approximately 90 percent of your liver is non-functioning by the time your doctor detects it. At that point you must severely curtail your drinking or possibly quit. Can you imagine the horror? Moreover, you will be told to follow a therapeutic liver diet that will make your life miserable.

If your hand started getting puffy and discolored from repeated contact with chemicals, you would take immediate steps to prevent further damage. Therefore, visualize alcohol as a chemical that irritates the liver, and realize each drink causes a little puffiness and color change to your liver.

It comes down to: "You can pay me now or you can pay me later, but you're gonna pay." The 21st Century Drinker opts to pay now in terms of learning to drink healthier. The reward is a lifetime of pure drinking enjoyment knowing that you have minimized your risk of being a health statistic. Cycle Drinking can be viewed as supplemental preventive health insurance for the 21st Century Drinker who consumes five or more drinks daily. Amateur Drinkers do not practice Cycle Drinking nor do they take life-force nutrients. They take their chances and end up crying in their drink when they develop alcohol-related health problems.

Cycle Drinking can be useful during periods when you will be drinking more than usual. For some this may mean the period between Thanksgiving Day and St. Patrick's Day, or during the dog days of summer. Furthermore, varying the type of alcohol you drink is also a component of Cycle Drinking. If you mainly drink straight hard liquor, you are more prone to developing disorders of the esophagus. The undiluted alcohol can erode the delicate lining of this structure and over time can give rise to ulcers and possibly cancer, especially if you use tobacco products. Cycle Drinking suggests that you rotate your choice of drinks. If you normally drink straight liquor, switch over to mixed drinks one week per month. Acquire a taste for wine or beer and enjoy them the next week. This should be easy after having acquired a taste for the hard stuff. This will enable the delicate mucous membranes that line your mouth, esophagus, and intestines to be bathed in varying strengths of alcohol rather than consistent 80 proof.

The Three Components to Cycle Drinking:

- One week out of each month reduce your daily intake by 50 percent — if your daily intake is a twelve-pack, you would limit your drinking to a six-pack per day for that week
- Two days out of each week limit your drinking to two drinks or less. It does not matter which two days you choose. The other five days of the week drink whatever you normally drink
- If you primarily drink hard liquor explore the vast world of wine and micro-brewed beer and substitute them for the hard stuff two weeks a month.

Learn what the 21st Century Drinker already knows, "A drink from the vine is healthy any time." Fermented beverages like wine and beer are gentler and healthier than their distilled cousins. Cycle Drinking allows you to drink every day and still rest your liver 104 out of the 365 days in the year.

Additionally, your liver will have eighty-four days when its workload is reduced by 50 percent.

The 21st Century Drinker does not find Cycle Drinking to be a hardship. A 21st Century Drinker understands that Cycle Drinking provides structure which is essential for any activity to have a successful outcome. In this case the outcome is a healthier body and enhanced quality of life. A practicing alcoholic who converts to a 21st Century Drinker may not want to or be able to follow Cycle Drinking. However, they could adopt a modified version of Cycle Drinking. This would be a decisive step towards drinking healthier and a welcomed change for the liver. Remember, the more you drink, especially if most of your drinking is from the hard stuff, the more your liver can benefit from Cycle Drinking. For the 21st Century Drinker, drinking is no longer a losing proposition.

Monthly Cycle Drinking Plan

	Sun	Mon	Tue	Wed	Thur	Fri	Sat
1st Week	Drink as Normal	Drink as Normal	2 Drinks or Less	Drink as Normal	2 Drinks or Less	Drink as Normal	Drink as Normal
2nd Week	Drink as Normal	Drink as Normal	2 Drinks or Less	2 Drinks or Less	Drink as Normal	Drink as Normal	Drink as Normal
3rd Week	Drink 50% of Normal	Drink 50% of Normal	Drink 50% of Normal	Drink 50% of Normal	Drink 50% of Normal	Drink 50% of Normal	Drink 50% of Normal
4th Week	Drink as Normal	Drink as Normal	2 Drinks or Less	2 Drinks or Less	Drink as Normal	Drink as Normal	Drink as Normal
5th Week	2 Drinks or Less	Drink as Normal	Drink as Normal	Drink as Normal	Drink as Normal	2 Drinks or Less	Drink as Normal

You can develop your own cycle. However, you must have **two 2 Drinks or Less days each week** except during the "Drink 50% of Normal" week, and **one entire week must be a Drink 50% of Normal week.**

	Sun	Mon	Tue	Wed	Thur	Fri	Sat
1st week							
2nd week							
3rd week							
4th week							
5th week							

Zone Drinking: Respecting the Body's Natural Cycle

The study of Chinese medicine reveals that each organ in the body has a time period when it is most active, and when it is least active or quiet. Interestingly, the liver is most quiet during the hours of 1:00 p.m. and 3:00 p.m. each day, and most active during the period from 1:00 a.m. to 3:00 a.m. This may explain why many cultures take a nap or siesta in the early afternoon.

Many people, myself included, experience a temporary lull in energy during the early afternoon. Since the liver is the primary organ for energy metabolism its lowered activity in the early afternoon could explain this phenomena. Therefore, if possible try to respect the body's natural cycle by drinking less during the liver's quiet period. It also makes a great 21st Century excuse for passing up a double martini at lunch time. Everyone will respect the intelligence of the 21st Century Drinker.

Intuitively and biochemically it makes sense that each organ system has a scheduled downtime. The hours of 1:00 a.m. to 3:00 a.m. are the high energy or active hours for the liver — a true blessing for the night time drinker. Anecdotal evidence seems to support that drinkers tend to plateau in terms of their buzz between 1:00 a.m. and 3:00 a.m. Possibly the liver can metabolize alcohol more efficiently during these hours. Zone drinking may be viewed as esoteric, but for the 21st Century Drinker it's a matter of being in total control and having full knowledge of how to drink healthier.

Prevention Can Pave the Road to a Lifetime of Healthier Drinking

Twentieth century nutritional biochemistry has yet to be applied as a solution to alcohol-related health problems. The medical community prefers to research new drugs to better manage disease and illness. After all, that is their focus, disease management rather than prevention of disease.

People with education in animal husbandry and veterinary science have a better grasp of supplement use than many physicians and dietitians. This is disturbing to me but I understand. Not because there is lack of financial gain in using preventive nutrition, but because preventive nutrition is not emphasized enough in medical school or nutrition degree programs. Do not take my comments here the wrong way, I respect physicians and dietitians. I have good friends who are one or the other. However, I would not rely on them to provide me with information on how to drink healthier. Neither should you. The only way you can drink healthier and live longer productively is to become a 21st Century Drinker.

At the twenty-first century, 100 million drinkers in the United States are oblivious to the fact that they could be drinking healthier. Have you ever been told that you can drink healthier? Probably not, and these are four reasons why: (1) Physicians do not know how to drink healthier; (2) People are so brainwashed into thinking alcohol is the scourge of mankind that they ignore the facts; (3) Too much medical talent is being devoted to weight loss books; (4) Too many dietitians still believe vitamin, mineral, anti-oxidant, lipotropic, and herbal supplements are unnecessary as long as you choose from the basic four food groups.

Over the last three years I studied the food diaries of 400 people ages 18-90 and 90 percent had inadequate intake of vitamins and minerals. It is easy to imagine illness raising its ugly head from such a fertile state of malnutrition, irrespective of the presence of alcohol. Too many people are trying to lose weight, eating on the run, and skipping meals. Moreover, too few are using nutritional supplements as preventive insurance. Even a non-drinker should view life-force nutrients like overdraft protection on a checking account. If food intake does not deposit enough vitamins, anti-oxidants, lipotropic factors, and minerals into the blood, the supplements cover the deficit, and their health remains in good standing.

The drinker should view supplements like mandatory automobile insurance. It's simple. You can never drive carefully enough that the need for insurance is unnecessary. Likewise, if you drink you can never eat well enough that the need for life-force nutrients is unnecessary. If you want to protect your car and financial assets you pay for insurance protection. If you want to protect your health, and preserve the ability to enjoy alcohol for a lifetime, you must follow the plan of a 21st Century Drinker. The 21st Century Drinker knows it is impossible to drink healthier without the use of life-force nutrients. He never leaves home without them.

The Future

There has been a shift in the way the drinker consumes alcohol. The idea of drinking healthier has arrived, and with it, a template for drinking healthier. There is no turning back. No longer can this fact be concealed from the drinker. Drinking healthier could not have been developed by a substance-abuse expert or anyone whose set of rules rejects this premise. Too many people view alcohol as being bad for them, and this viewpoint arrests their ability to see beyond abstinence. Alcohol is neither good nor bad. It is simply alcohol. We could say people are good or bad. However, more accurately, they are informed or uninformed.

Many drinkers will greatly benefit from my model of drinking healthier. The principles of 21st Century Drinking are long overdue. I saved myself, and many others, a world of future heartache and pain, not to mention a great deal of expense, by developing a way to drink healthier. Moreover, my drinking will never be a liability to anyone, and this includes the government-administered Medicare program. Becoming a 21st Century Drinker through drinking healthier is a solution to the staggering annual health care cost of treating alcohol-related illness. In the older population alone more than a million people have a problem with alcohol. Seventy percent of hospital admissions of older people in 1991 were for alcohol-related health problems. Alcohol-related problems put more older Americans in the hospital than heart attacks. Malnutrition and the overall lack of life-force nutrients are responsible for their need of modern medicine.

By becoming a 21st Century Drinker middle-aged and older drinkers can protect their health and stay out of the hospital. What's more importantly, drinking healthier will prevent today's younger drinkers from being tomorrow's health-care problem. This alone should make our policy makers crane their necks for a peek at *Drink as Much As You Want and Live Longer.*

Liver Protection: The Use of Herbs, Lipotropic Factors, Anti-Oxidants, Protein, and Water

All sorts of body diseases are produced by half-used minds. — George Bernard Shaw

Each swallow of alcohol is like a small fire your liver has to extinguish before it spreads throughout the body. The chemicals used to put out the fire are life-force nutrients. If they are not available your health will suffer. Life-force nutrients help protect the liver so the liver can protect you. If you knew all the special functions your liver performs daily you would be startled — they are functions only the liver can perform, functions you cannot live without!

If you knew how often your liver is attacked by toxic "enemies" you would make every attempt to protect it from future harm. The liver's special functions are impressive, and its enemies are plentiful, silent, and deadly. This should convince you that liver protection is essential for the drinker and worthy of consideration by the non-drinker.

Special Functions Performed by the Liver

- Filters one quart of blood per minute and neutralizes enemy toxins
- Packages enemy toxins in bile and sends them to the gallbladder for excretion
- Produces bile that functions to absorb vitamins and essential fats
- Filters cholesterol from the blood and excretes it along with enemy toxins
- Collects nutrients from the intestines and sends them to hungry cells without delay
- Stores nutrients for use during sleep and other periods when the body has no food
- Stores glycogen (sugar) and makes sugars, fats, proteins, and lipotropic factors
- Makes the protein responsible for clotting blood and forming bone
- Makes protective proteins that maintain health and enable the body to heal itself
- Activates a "calcium helper" which allows the intestines to absorb calcium

Enemies That Attack Your Liver

- All forms of alcohol: beer, wine, champagne, sangria, coolers, and spirits
- Acetaldehyde: a by-product of alcohol processing that must be processed too
- Arsenic and cyanide: inhaled when smoking or breathing second-hand smoke
- Air pollution: lead, sulfur dioxide, ozone, carbon monoxide, and nitrogen dioxide
- Anabolic steroids: commonly used by athletes to enhance muscle mass
- Aluminum-containing antacids: used for indigestion and heartburn
- Asbestos: found in some older buildings
- Burned or charred meat: may contain cancer-causing substances
- Bacteria: that enter the intestines or other entrances into the body
- Industrial chemicals: inhaled or absorbed through the skin
- Ingestion of toxins, drugs, and growth hormones: found in animal liver
- Herbicides: 600,000 tons produced yearly in the U.S.
- Pesticides
- Free-radicals: unstable molecules generated in the body during normal metabolic reactions. They will damage tissues, organs and cells if the body lacks anti-oxidants.
- Drug-hormones: to speed growth found in beef and poultry products

- Mercury, aluminum, lead, and cadmium: found in water, cigarette smoke, cookware, lead crystal, and batteries leaking their contents into our environment
- Obesity and high-fat diets: contribute to a fatty liver
- Oral contraceptives
- Prescription drugs
- Street drugs
- Tylenol, ibuprofen, acetaminophen, and other over the counter pain medications
- Viruses that cause hepatitis and cirrhosis

The Idea of Liver Insurance Protection

Visualize your liver as a protective filter embedded with life-force nutrients that nourish the liver and help neutralize alcohol and other "enemies" before they can cause damage. The liver also utilizes life-force nutrients to accomplish its many special functions. However, when toxic enemies are present, the liver is forced to divert the flow of nutrients away from special functions and towards battling the enemy. The liver places itself in harm's way, battles the enemy, and emerges victorious when a sufficient stock of life-force nutrients is available. Since it's impossible to damage your liver permanently during brief periods of riotous drinking, the liver appears to have the ability to heal itself with its storage of proper nutrients.

At some point all drinkers more or less started off with adequate liver protection; however, failure to replace these nutrients over the years results in liver damage or a "clogged" filter. Unless you receive a liver transplant you cannot replace the filter when it becomes damaged. Therefore, it is essential that you take preventive measures to ensure your liver has sufficient life-force nutrients to continually self-clean, nourish cells, and win future drinking bouts. No drinker is too young or too old for liver insurance. It's like investing in stocks: the earlier you start the better off financially you will be later in life.

Insurance is a familiar concept to most people. We routinely protect ourselves, our family, and our valuables from loss or damage by purchasing insurance plans. Our decision to purchase insurance is based on the cost, likelihood of the loss occurring, and how much we stand to lose if an accident or loss occurs. Some insurance decisions are straightforward like the purchase of car theft and homeowner's insurance. Since most of us could not afford to replace a stolen car or stolen home furnishings and jewelry, we choose to purchase theft insurance protection.

However, if we want to minimize the chances of a loss we install an alarm system. Why? Because theft insurance does not prevent the loss from occurring, it only helps replace whatever is stolen. The beauty of liver insurance is it's really a preventive maintenance plan. We all know that an ounce of prevention is worth a pound of cure and this applies to drinking.

Drinking healthier coats the liver cells with life-force nutrient protection and minimizes the chances of liver damage. You may have been told that food provides all the nutrition you need to stay healthy. Well, friends, let me tell you the truth. Having that belief is like wearing a paper raincoat in a storm. Alcohol is the storm and if your only protection is the paper raincoat provided by food, you will end up sick. It is impossible to obtain the necessary amounts of life-force nutrient protection from food, just as it's impossible to protect your home by just closing the doors.

In comparison to the priceless value of your health, life-force nutrient protection is cheap, and the likelihood of needing this protection is 100 percent each time you belly up to the bar. Life-force nutrient protection is necessary insurance for a drinker, just as wearing a helmet is necessary insurance for a motorcyclist. If I decided to ride a motorcycle, I would never say, "Forget the helmet. I have medical insurance." We know that medical insurance does not prevent head injury. The risk of head injury only decreases by wearing a helmet and riding carefully. It is our responsibility to take the same precautionary measures to keep our liver healthy while drinking. Smart motorcyclists wear a helmet to protect their heads, smart homeowners protect their homes with an alarm system, and 21st Century Drinkers protect their livers with a coating of life-force nutrients.

In the final analysis, life-force nutrient protection is healthful, relatively inexpensive, offers peace of mind, minimizes the chances of liver disease, and reduces the need to utilize costly medical insurance. Your liver is more valuable than anything you currently protect with insurance; doesn't it make sense to start protecting your liver today? Furthermore, the cost for a "donor" transplanted liver, if one is available in your time of need, would exceed the value of most homes!

Assessing Your Odds of Liver Disease

How often do you ingest or come into contact with liver enemies? Only you can answer that question, but I would guess it is more often than you think. The list of liver enemies should provoke the question, "If an individual develops liver damage and also happens to be a drinker, was alcohol the cause of the damage or could one or more of the enemies alone or in combination with alcohol be responsible?"

Make check marks next to the "enemies" you come in frequent contact with. I would bet you will mark no less than ten, and that's if you are living a quite saintly life. One hundred sixty-four million Americans reside in cities and towns that do not meet the National Ambient Air Quality Standards for air pollution. They live, breathe, eat, work, and play in a virtual sewer of pollutants. Tell me this has no effect on their liver and overall health. Drinkers are exposed daily to many of the liver enemies, all of which are toxins comparable to or worse than alcohol. However, many of the enemies are not completely understood and are difficult to measure or see.

Because of the invisible nature of these enemies, they are causally brushed off as factors in the development of liver damage. Since alcohol is highly visible and can cause deviant behavior as readily as euphoria, it becomes the vilified enemy. When you lack life-force nutrients and live in an environment filled with toxins, your liver becomes a playground for the enemy rather than the place of death! It's that simple.

Normal Food Cannot Provide Adequate Liver Protection

If normal food could protect the liver and immune system from alcohol damage we wouldn't be witnessing the deaths and morbidity that result as a consequence of drinking. End of story. The average drinker is deficient in a number of vitamins, lipotropic factors, anti-oxidants, and minerals. Most clients I have worked with over the last ten years do not consume the Recommended Dietary Allowances (RDA) of vitamins and minerals set by the United States government. They too were walking around in paper raincoats. This is not shocking since most people make poor food choices, eat on the run, skip breakfast or lunch or both, and rely on dinner to balance everything out. By drinking unprotected and consuming only one or two meals a day, you are just begging for a health problem.

My research indicates most people do not eat well enough to stay healthy in a non-toxic fairy-tale world where alcohol and the other enemies are non-existent. Therefore, it is not surprising in the toxic world in which we live that alcohol becomes the straw that breaks the camel's back.

Most people are only beginning to explore the world of herbal and nutritional treatments for disease and health maintenance. Better late than never. However, medical professionals are still behind the learning curve in this area and are inadequately prepared to offer the much needed guidance. Most health professionals have forgotten about the biochemical functions of vitamins, lipotropic factors, anti-oxidants, and minerals or how they enable the liver to process alcohol. Some know little beyond what the RDA states.

Moreover, since there is no RDA for herbs, lipotropic factors, and some anti-oxidants, it's assumed that normal food will provide an adequate supply. This could not be further from the truth. The thought that a simple and inexpensive herb or nutrient could have a protective effect and not have an established RDA is beyond the comprehension of some health professionals. They were taught that herbs and nutrient supplementation are a form of quackery and the RDA is the only gospel.

The fact is, herbal medicine has been around for 5,000 years and is a proven science. Millions of herbal practitioners have learned to unlock the power of nature and direct it towards self healing, therefore preventing the need for modern medicine. Of course there are times when there is no substitute for modern medicine, but too often we rely on modern medicine to treat conditions that should never occur in the first place. For instance, alcohol-related health problems are largely due to preventable nutrient deficiencies. The health consequences of these deficiencies are so devastating that modern medicine is needed to salvage the drinker.

The RDAs are still in their infancy and leave much to be desired. They do not recognize deficiencies that are impending, such as those which develop in the drinker, nor do they consider special requirements that are not among the current RDAs. The RDAs are still evolving and I hope one day they will reflect the nutritional requirements for drinking healthier. I know the RDA folks have vision because they set the RDAs higher for pregnant women because the growing fetus drains the mother's nutrient stores. All they need to do now is harness this vision and realize that alcohol drains the drinker of nutrients in the same way as the growing fetus drains its mother. Case closed. Verdict: Drinkers are discriminated against once again!

What Are Free Radicals and How Do They Damage Cells?

What exactly are free radicals and how does liver insurance protect our cells from their damage?

This will require a little chemistry to answer. Free radicals are molecules that have unpaired electrons in their outer shell causing them to be unstable or restless. They are formed during normal "oxidation" reactions such as exercise, illness, digestion, metabolism, and healing. The unpaired electrons want a partner so they can become stable and settle down, no different than our desire to go peacefully through life with a loving partner. Without paired electrons these molecules have too much energy and bounce around and try to strip an electron from any unsuspecting cell membrane.

house and how it protects the contents of your house. The cell membrane is like a roof that protects the inside of the cell. To better visualize a free radical and the damaging effect it causes, think of a bolt of lightning striking your roof. Free radicals are like mini-lightning bolts that zap each cell in the body 10,000 times per day causing cellular damage.

Cell membranes are made of liquid fats and other nutrients that possess electrons that are wanted by the free radical. Once the free radical steals an electron from the cell membrane it causes the cell membrane to become unstable and leaky. The cell membrane is no longer able to effectively protect the inner contents of the cell and the cell leaks out critical factors required for survival. Moreover, unwanted substances can now enter the cell and create "cell chaos."

Free radicals also attack proteins and DNA, which contains your genetic code. All told, free radicals are nothing but trouble. However, alcohol always brings these "friends" when it comes to your party!

Common Circumstances That Can Stimulate Free-Radical Development

- Alcohol and acetaldehyde processing
- Normal metabolic reactions that use oxygen
- Healing
- Infections
- Exercise
- Having too much body fat
- Tobacco use or inhaling second-hand smoke
- Too much iron
- Sunbathing
- Air pollution
- Breathing oxygen from oxygen tanks

What Are Anti-oxidants
and How Do They Kill Free Radicals
Before Damage Occurs?

To visualize an anti-oxidant think of how a lightning rod protects a tall building. The lightning rod absorbs the electrical blow instead of the building or roof. Anti-oxidants are like mini-lightning rods floating inside and around your cells trying to attract free radicals. Anti-oxidants are "electron donors" who stand in the way and sacrifice themselves in order to protect the cell membranes and cholesterol. The free radical accepts the electron from the anti-oxidant and the damage is prevented. Anti-oxidants are valuable foot soldiers in the battle against alcohol and its by-product acetaldehyde.

Therefore, it is essential that the drinker arm the liver with the power of anti-oxidants to minimize liver cell damage. Unprotected liver cells are killed by free radicals and this cell "death" impairs the liver's ability to perform its special functions. Based on nutrient intake studies I have performed, many drinkers obtain insufficient quantities of anti-oxidants from their food. Therefore, supplements are required to protect the liver.

Anti-oxidants: Weapons Against Disease!

Vitamin E. A fat-soluble vitamin that protects cellular membranes from free-radical damage. Vitamin E enhances the power of two other anti-oxidants called glutathione and selenium. Anti-oxidants are added to margarine, butter, and vegetable oil to prevent the oil from being attacked by free-radical oxidation. Oxygen can attack fats causing them to become rancid or rotten. This oxidation is similar to what happens inside your body when free radicals attack unprotected fat-cell membranes and cell membranes of all other tissues. Obese individuals have more fat to protect and require additional vitamin E. A high-fat diet also increases the need for vitamin E. If it's important enough to add anti-oxidants to bottles of oil, doesn't it make sense to supplement your diet with vitamin E too?

Vitamin C. A water soluble vitamin that functions as an anti-oxidant when the body is fighting "enemies." The immune system uses a considerable amount of oxygen when it is fighting off an infection. This process produces free radicals that can damage unprotected cells. Vitamin C is also required for amino-acid metabolism, formation of protective liver proteins, and is necessary for proper wound healing.

Glutathione. A tri-amino acid made of glycine, cysteine, and glutamate. Glutathione neutralizes free radicals that damage cell membranes and DNA. Glutathione is a building block for the powerful glutathione peroxidase enzyme responsible for killing free radicals. Glutathione peroxidase contains the building block selenium and requires zinc in order to be active. Methionine is needed to make the cysteine used in the production of glutathione. Vitamin E enhances the power of glutathione peroxidase. These interrelationships should make it clear that relying on the four food groups is inadequate protection for the drinker.

Selenium. An essential trace mineral known for its anti-oxidant activity and necessary for normal pancreatic function. Drinkers who are deficient in selenium may develop pancreatic insufficiency, which means the pancreas does not release adequate digestive enzymes and buffering solution into the recycling plant. This results in poor separation of nutrients from food as discussed in Chapter 1. Vitamin E protects selenium cycling plant. This results in poor separation of nutrients from food as discussed in Chapter 1. Vitamin E protects selenium from being damaged or lost from the body. Selenium is required to manufacture the powerful glutathione peroxidase enzyme.

How to Cleanse the Liver and Lymph Fluid: The Use of Herbs and Water-Soluble Fiber

During the liver's battle with enemy toxins, harmful substances clog the liver and lymph. Herbs and sulfur compounds are required to clear the liver and lymph fluid. Lymph fluid carries fats and fat soluble vitamins from the intestines (recycling plant) to the bloodstream, bypassing the liver. Since it bypasses the filtering process in the liver, it is important that the lymph fluid is purified before it empties into the blood supply. Herbs and sulfur are "fiber" for your liver and lymph, just as bran is fiber for your colon. Both have a healthful cleansing effect.

How do herbs protect the liver? Herbs help prevent a condition called cholestasis, which occurs when bile flow within the liver or from the liver to the gallbladder is slowed or blocked completely. When bile, which can be viewed as liver "feces," becomes trapped within or outside the liver cells it causes liver "constipation" or congestion. This results in sluggishness and prevents the liver from neutralizing "enemies" efficiently or performing its other special functions. This inability to neutralize allows any "enemy" to gain entrance into the body and inflict damage.

Why does the bile become trapped? Probably from fat accumulating in the liver, and free-radical damage that killed liver cells that normally facilitated the flow of bile. Liver fat compresses the normal cells and cuts off the flow of bile, just like clothing leaving a "congestion" line from poor blood circulation.

Therefore, it is important that the drinker minimizes fatty infiltration of the liver, sluggish flow of bile, and free radical damage. Lipotropic factors can help the liver remove fat buildup and decrease the likelihood of the fat from ever being deposited. If an individual has cirrhosis, hepatitis, or fatty liver, lipotropic factors and herbs are needed to help heal the liver. Lipotropic factors are discussed later in the chapter.

Herbs That Protect the Liver

Herbs such as goldenseal and echinacea help strengthen the immune system. This is extremely important for drinkers because alcohol weakens the immune system. Drinkers who become sick tend to take longer to recover. The weakened liver is unable to make the special healing and defense proteins required for fast recovery. Certain herbs strengthen liver-cell function and improve the ability to make disease-fighting proteins.

Other herbs can stimulate new liver cell growth, cleanse bile and lymph, and improve the circulation of both blood and lymph. Lymph fluid washes through areas of the body that are lined with little bacteria killing "factories" and at times these factories or "lymph nodes" become infected and swollen, impeding the flow of lymph and creating a state of mild or severe lymph "constipation."

Recall that bile is liver "feces." Certain herbs stimulate the excretion of bile from the liver. The need to keep bile and lymph flowing properly and pure is no different than the need to keep your bowels moving and clear. The following herbs strengthen the immunity, liver cells, circulation of blood and lymph, and promote growth of new cells.

Milk Thistle *(Silybum marianum)*. German pharmaceutical companies use milk thistle in a number of drugs used to treat liver congestion, fatty liver, hepatitis, and cirrhosis of the liver. Milk thistle acts like an anti-oxidant and kills free radicals while protecting glutathione from being destroyed. Moreover, milk thistle is known to increase protein synthesis, which enables the liver to make new cells. Milk thistle helps the liver trap enemies that have entered the body from the recycling plant (intestines) or other portal of entry. Milk thistle is considered by many to be the number-one herb of choice when it comes to protecting the liver from toxic enemy damage and impaired bile flow. Improved bile flow allows the liver to excrete toxic metals such as aluminum, mercury, cadmium, arsenic, and others.

Dandelion Root *(Taraxacum officinale)*. Most people think of dandelions as annoying and useless weeds that invade the lawn. However, dandelion has profound beneficial effects on the liver and gallbladder. Dandelion stimulates the liver to release bile to the gallbladder, a bile storage organ. It also stimulates the flow of bile from the gallbladder to the intestines (recycling plant) where it is needed to emulsify fats and absorb vitamins A, D, E, and K. The constant flow of bile prevents gallstone formation, liver congestion, and dysfunction. Dandelion would be beneficial for anyone with liver congestion, fatty liver, hepatitis, or cirrhosis of the liver. Dandelion can also help lower cholesterol and act as an anti-inflammatory agent in the bile duct and liver cell. The anti-inflammatory effect may help prevent pancreatitis caused by digestive enzymes regurgitating back into the pancreas because they were unable to pass down the swollen duct. Dandelion also contains vitamins and minerals and is a rich source of choline. Never refuse a glass of homemade dandelion wine.

Artichokes *(Cynara scolymus)*. Artichokes improve the flow of bile from the liver to the gallbladder and increase cell growth. They can lower cholesterol levels by stimulating the liver to release cholesterol-laden bile to the gallbladder for excretion into the intestines.

Cayenne Pepper *(Capsicum anuum)*. A potent vasodilator that warms the whole body and improves blood flow to all organs. This is important for the efficient transportation of life-force nutrients. Refer to Chapter 10 for drink recipes that have the added zing of cayenne pepper. If you have poor circulation in your hands and feet, cayenne pepper can help this condition, too. The ultimate liver treatment is artichokes sprinkled with cayenne pepper chased down with a glass of dandelion wine.

Goldenseal *(Hydrastis canadensis)*. A well-researched herb that helps purify the lymph and blood. Goldenseal helps the healing process by stimulating new cell growth. When I worked in an alcohol and drug rehabilitation program, the clients told me how to use goldenseal to remove traces of drugs from the urine. They used this method to pass drug screenings given at work!

Echinacea *(Echinacea angustifolia)*. Fortifies the immune system by activating white blood cells and other immune cells responsible for killing bacteria. This is a good herb for preventing colds and flu and should be taken at the first sign of feeling sick. I have had a great deal of success boosting immunity with a combination of goldenseal, echinacea, burdock root, and vitamin C. The drinker benefits from echinacea's ability to help the liver defend itself against toxic enemies. A number of well-researched books have been written on echinacea.

Water-Soluble Fiber. Any fiber that becomes gummy when cooked or chewed. Good sources are cooked oatmeal, barley, bananas, legumes, and fruits. Crunchy fiber from vegetables, bran, wheat, and other grains are insoluble fiber and are not as effective. However, they are needed to prevent constipation. Other names for water-soluble fiber are pectin, psyllium, oat bran, and guar gum. Because fiber is not absorbed by the body it makes an excellent vehicle for binding and eliminating harmful substances.

After a night of drinking, the bile in the intestinal tract is loaded with toxic wastes and cholesterol. Water-soluble fiber can bind these harmful toxins and prevent them from being re-absorbed. The sticky nature of water soluble fiber also binds and eliminates bacteria and yeast found in the intestinal tract, and mutated bile that was created by intestinal bacteria. Mutated bile and charred meat are believed to be possible cancer-causing agents. However, both can be trapped in the sticky fiber and eliminated in the stool.

How to Minimize the Development of Fatty Liver and Cirrhosis: The Use of Lipotropic Factors

For decades most dietitians and physicians have declared lipotropic factors as "unnecessary" in terms of the need to supplement the diet. Their reasoning was that lipotropic factors are made in the body. Therefore, the body will always have a ready supply and can never become deficient. This reasoning could not be more faulty when applied to the drinker or anyone who engages the company of liver "enemies." True, the body can make lipotropic factors. However, drinkers often lack the necessary building blocks. Moreover, lipotropic factors are made in the liver; if the liver is damaged lipotropic factors cannot be produced. Therefore, drinkers should supplement their diets with pre-formed lipotropic factors.

Carnitine. A nitrogen-containing chemical formed in healthy liver from the essential amino acids lysine and methionine. These amino acids cannot be made in the body and must be provided from either protein rich foods or amino acid supplements. A deficiency of B6, B12, or folate will block the formation of carnitine in the liver.

Carnitine is needed to carry fat to the fat-burning center of the liver cell. This shuttling prevents fat from accumulating in the liver.

Pharmaceutical companies add carnitine to special liquid formulas designed to treat patients with liver damage. Therefore, it is reasonable to recommend that drinkers supplement carnitine to enable their liver to properly burn fat.

Methionine. An essential amino acid containing sulfur. Methionine is activated in the liver and used mainly to produce other substances critical to the health of the drinker. When the liver is fighting alcohol or other enemies, methionine is used to make two amino acids, cysteine and taurine, which help the liver neutralize toxic enemies. Taurine, a building block of bile, is made from cysteine.

Many of the liver enemies are fat soluble and will embed themselves in cell membranes and avoid being filtered out of the body by the liver and kidney. Cysteine and taurine attack and bind these enemies, changing them into water-soluble forms which can then be excreted from the body in the urine. Methionine is used to make lecithin and can help prevent poor bile flow caused by alcohol, acetaldehyde, oral contraceptives, anabolic steroids, and other "enemies" listed earlier. Oral contraceptives alter liver cell membranes, causing a change in how cells receive and release bile. Methionine is needed to properly form DNA; improperly formed DNA can cause cancer development.

Choline. Manufactured in the "healthy" liver from the amino acids serine and methionine in the presence of vitamin B6, B12, and folate. Drinkers are often unable to make choline due to the lack of the above vitamins and amino acids. Choline comes from the French word *chole,* which means bile. If the drinker lacks choline the body cannot make lecithin.

Lecithin. A natural fat emulsifier found in bile. Lecithin is used to form cell membranes, and is used in the lipoproteins that transport fat and cholesterol to and from the liver and tissues. Lecithin allows bile to remain fluid, preventing liver "constipation" and cholesterol gallstones. It protects liver cells from scarring during their contact with acetaldehyde, a toxin formed during alcohol processing. An individual who already has excessive scarring (fibrosis) or cirrhosis would benefit from lecithin. Lecithin also restores the activity of a protein called cytochrome which is needed to capture energy from food.

Zinc: An Overlooked Mineral

Zinc deficiency is widespread in this country and little action has been taken to address this problem. This fact is especially alarming since adequate zinc is critical to the well-being of the drinker. Zinc is needed to activate the "neutralizing" enzymes required to process alcohol into a non-toxic compound. Zinc deficiency affects DNA and protein manufacturing, impairs the body's ability to defend itself against infections, and delays wound healing.

Red meat is the richest source of absorbable zinc and as individuals reduce their beef intake, zinc intake falls too. A 1985 study showed the average red meat consumption by women provided only 20 percent of the RDA for zinc. Male and female drinkers need supplemental zinc at all levels of consumption,

and drinkers who are vegetarians need it the most. Zinc and B6
are required to activate hundreds of enzymes and are required
for proper testicular, immune, and liver function.

How to Determine Your Protein Intake and Daily Protein Needs

Adequate protein is needed to repair and build new cells.
Without protein, all is lost. No other life-force nutrient
provides the nitrogen needed for growth and repair. Chronic
drinking increases the amount of protein lost in the pancreatic
juices released during the processing of food and alcohol.
Therefore, it is important to consume the correct amount of
protein to replace losses and repair tissue damage. Most
drinkers do not know how much protein they are consuming or
their daily requirements. Because we do not have to be precise,
the following table should allow you to determine your
approximate protein intake for a 24-hour period.

Protein Source	Amount	Grams of Protein (g)	Example
Egg	One large	7	2 eggs = 14g
Meat, fowl, fish	1 oz.	7	4 oz. burger = 28g
Beans, legumes	½ cup	7	1 cup chili = 14g
Cheese	1 oz.	7	3 oz. piece = 21g
Milk	1 oz.	1	8 oz. glass = 8g
Ice cream	½ cup	3	1 cup = 6g
Peanut butter	2 tablespoons	8	1 tablespoon = 4g
Vegetables	1/2 cup	2	1 cup broccoli = 4g
Bread and starches	1 slice or 1/2 cup starch	3	English muffin = 6g 1 cup rice = 6g

The amount of protein that your body requires to stay healthy depends on your physical size. All drinkers should consume close to the levels shown below.

If your weight is	Female (wt x 0.7) up to 175 pounds	Male (wt x 0.8)	Additional protein needed per drink*
100 pounds	70 grams protein	80 grams protein	3 grams protein
125 pounds	88 grams protein	100 grams protein	3 grams protein
150 pounds	105 grams protein	120 grams protein	4 grams protein
175 pounds	123 grams protein	140 grams protein	4 grams protein
200 pounds	123 grams protein	160 grams protein	4 grams protein
225 pounds	133 grams protein	170 grams protein	4 grams protein
250 pounds	133 grams protein	170 grams protein	5 grams protein
275 pounds	143 grams protein	170 grams protein	5 grams protein
300 pounds	143 grams protein	170 grams protein	6 grams protein
To calculate your protein needs based on your exact weight	Your weight in pounds x 0.7 = grams of protein	Your weight in pounds x 0.8 = grams of protein	Choose the row that is closest to your weight. Example, 140 pounds = 4 grams protein per drink. If you drink 4 drinks (4 x 4 = 16g)

* Always try to consume the additional protein per drink, especially if you are unable to consume the protein amount listed for your weight.

Choosing the Right Protein Source to Prevent a Fatty Liver

Low Fat Protein Sources	How To Prepare It
Eggs with or without nonfat Healthy Choice shredded cheese	Teflon pan with no oil, butter, margarine, or nonstick spray
Nonfat yogurt	Open container and use a spoon
Grilled nonfat cheese sandwich	Oven/toaster, grill or use Teflon pan as above
Grilled skinless chicken breasts	Marinate in wine, add garlic and onion powder, balsamic vinegar, salt & pepper
Pork tenderloin (high in B1)	Grill or pan fry in fat-free Italian dressing
Beef eye-round or beef tips (high in zinc)	Grill or pan fry in red wine and fat-free Italian or French dressing, add garlic, salt & pepper
Albacore or chunk light tuna in water	Use 1 tsp. light mayonnaise per 6 oz. can tuna, add diced celery and pickles
Shellfish	Grill or steam. Clams and oysters can be consumed raw, but be sure to use plenty of fresh lemon.
Lobster and shrimp	Steamed or broiled, serve with cocktail sauce and lemon
McDonald's fajita chicken salad	Let them prepare it for you
Any fish except salmon	Grill or pan fry as above, use white wine instead of red
Turkey breast	Buy it sliced at a deli or cook an entire turkey. Good for sandwiches or for omelets
Hardee's grilled chicken salad or sandwich	Ask for fat-free salad dressing
Burger King BK broiler chicken sandwich	Ask them to hold the mayo sauce
Wendy's grilled chicken fillet sandwich	Let them prepare it for you
Subway turkey, ham, or roast beef	Ask them to hold the salad oil and mayo
Carl's Jr. chicken breast salad	Ask for the nonfat dressing

Most drinkers need to add protein to their diets. However, many protein foods are high in fat and can contribute to obesity and fatty liver. Therefore, it is important that you choose low fat protein sources as often as possible. Of course you can still eat high fat favorites like Italian sausage or corned beef, but not every day. Most low fat cheeses and yogurt are quite good and you can acquire a taste for skim milk just as easily as alcohol. All it takes is practice, so try to choose the low fat or nonfat versions the next time you reach for dairy. The table below will help you make better protein decisions. Your liver is depending on you to make the right choices most of the time.

How to Figure Out Your Water Needs So You Can Drink Healthier!

Water needs are based on your body size and percentage of muscle tissue. Muscular individuals require more water since muscle tissue is mostly water.

Many drinkers are chronically dehydrated and this hinders the ability of the liver and kidneys to excrete toxic waste formed during the processing of alcohol and other liver enemies. Part A is the amount of water or liquid needed each day whether you drink alcohol or not. Part B is the amount of *additional water* required on drinking days.

Part A	Part B
You need 5 ounces of water or other non-alcohol liquid for every 10 pounds of body weight. This amount is needed every day whether you drink or not.	You need to drink an extra 3 ounces of *water* for each alcohol drink consumed
Example: A drinker weighs 150 pounds. How much water is needed daily? **150 pounds divided by 10 pounds = 15** **15 x 5 ounces = 75 ounces**	Example: The 150-pound drinker consumes 7 drinks during the day. How much extra **water** is needed? **7 drinks x 3 ounces = 21 ounces**

In the above example, the drinker must drink a total of 96 ounces of non-alcohol liquids. The amount from Part A can come from juice, water, and caffeine-free soda.

The amount from Part B must come from *plain water*. Moreover, the amount from Part B should be consumed during or after drinking and not before. This is very important!

Putting It All Together

Twenty-First Century Drinking requires knowledge and planning. You are developing an appreciation of how important life-force nutrients are to your overall health. Moreover, you understand that the basic four food groups cannot supply the nutrients your liver needs to process alcohol, and to keep you healthy. In the next chapter you will learn how and when to take the life-force nutrients.

How to Prepare Your Body for Its Meeting With Alcohol

The nature of man is always the same; it is their habits that separate them. — Confucius

Preparing your body for its meeting with alcohol is the crux of drinking healthier. As you already know this will require planning, planning, and planning, but earlier chapters have taught you that this is time well spent. At this point you are ready to implement the drinking healthier protection plan. How much and how often you need to take life-force nutrients depends on how much and how often you drink.

There are three levels and two sub-levels of life-force nutrient protection, each based on a specific range of alcohol consumption. The number of drinks dictate the type and amount of the life-force nutrients required to drink healthier.

Level II has a sub-level IIa, as does Level III which has sub-level IIIa. These sub-levels are part of a monthly rotation plan for level II and III drinkers who drink daily.

The Three Levels of Drinking Healthier

Level	Number of drinks consumed	Do I need to supplement *before* drinking?	Do I need to supplement *during* drinking?	Do I need to supplement *after* drinking?	Sub-level (simplified version)
I	1-3	Yes	No	Yes	No
II	4-9	Yes	No	Yes	Yes, IIa
III	10 or more	Yes	Yes	Yes	Yes, IIIa

I designed the three levels of life-force nutrient protection to take into consideration the unique nutrient demands of progressively higher intakes of alcohol. Clearly, the occasional drinker does not require the level of life-force nutrients needed by the drinker who often drinks greater quantities. However, if an occasional drinker decides to drink two more than usual he or she can follow the appropriate level for that drinking session. Likewise, a regular drinker who decides to drink "less" during a period of Cycle Drinking or for any other reason, can go down a level. The sub-levels are designed to replace those life-force nutrients that are more rapidly depleted. Moreover, it allows the drinker to follow a simplified version of their level for fourteen days out of each twenty-eight-day period without sacrificing protection.

The levels of drinking healthier are a blueprint for building and strengthening the body, enabling it to withstand the "body blows" that are packed into each drop of alcohol. Consuming the life-force nutrients for your level of drinking will help protect your body from free radical damage, premature aging, impaired immunity, and organ dysfunction that result when cells are exposed to alcohol. If there is a will there is a way, and each of us must decide on our own that drinking healthier is worth the effort and expense. Drinking healthier is a healthful habit that can replace "unhealthy" drinking practices.

Your loved ones (shareholders) have a vested interest in your living to be a ripe old age and they deserve nothing less, so neither should you. You have learned to get up each day and follow your own routine. It's never too late to make a slight adjustment to accommodate the practice of drinking healthier.

If you do not like taking pills, buy chewable or liquid nutrients when possible. Ask the salesperson at your local health food store if any of the life-force nutrients come in chewable or liquid forms. When you take the life-force nutrients visualize them replenishing each cell with the nutrition required to keep you healthy throughout a lifetime of drinking.

The three levels of life-force nutrient protection transform the act of drinking into a skillful strategy. The strategy and the protection it offers is only as strong as your ability to adhere to it. There are no short cuts or one magic pill that will provide you with the protection required to drink healthier.

The following table was introduced in Chapter 4 and is reprinted here to allow you to conveniently calculate your water needs. Remember, water is a life-force nutrient!

Part A	Part B
You need 5 ounces of water or other non-alcohol liquid for every 10 pounds of body weight. This amount is needed every day whether you drink or not.	You need to drink an extra 3 ounces of *water* for each alcohol drink consumed
Example: A drinker weighs 150 pounds. How much water is needed daily? **150 pounds divided by 10 pounds = 15** **15 x 5 ounces = 75 ounces**	Example: The 150-pound drinker consumes 7 drinks during the day. How much extra **water** is needed? **7 drinks x 3 ounces = 21 ounces**

Part A is the baseline fluid requirements for the average healthy person. If you have congestive heart failure or a kidney condition please consult your physician. Part B helps replace the cellular water lost during alcohol processing and should be consumed *during* or *after* drinking.

Level I   Life-Force Nutrient Protection

Life-force nutrients required when drinking 1-3 drinks	Amount	*Take before drinking	Actual time or meal that you will take the life-force nutrient	Take within 2 hours after drinking, no food required
Multi-vitamin	one tablet			✓
B-Complex with vitamin C added	one capsule	✓		
Vitamin E	400 IU	✓		
Mega or high-potency multi-minerals	one capsule	✓		
Milk thistle, dandelion, and artichoke combined in one capsule	475 mg	✓		
Water	Use water chart to calculate Part A & B	____oz. from Part A		____oz. from Part B

* Take anytime *before* drinking, preferably with food. You may also take them all at once or spread them among a few meals. Avoid taking the multi-minerals when consuming coffee, tea, or high fiber cereal.

Question: I drink one to three drinks twice a week. Can I follow Level I on my non-drinking days?

Answer: Yes, I strongly urge you to follow Level I daily. It will cover any nutritional deficiencies in your diet, and the inevitable nutrient loss caused by liver enemies. However, if your diet is perfectly balanced, follow Level I only when you will be drinking.

Question: Why should I avoid caffeine and high fiber cereal when taking minerals?

Answer: Both caffeine and fiber bind minerals and prevent their absorption. Caffeine acts a diuretic and causes the body to lose valuable cell water via urination.

Question: Can I substitute soda or juice for the water calculated in Part B above?

Answer: Drink plain water for Part B. Part A can be a mix of any type of non-alcohol liquid, but, water, carbonated flavored water, juice, and caffeine-free diet soda are your best choices.

Level II   Life-Force Nutrient Protection

Life-force nutrients required when drinking 4-9 drinks	Amount	*Take anytime before drinking	Record the time that you will take the life-force nutrient	Take again within 2 hours after drinking, or during drinking, no food required
B-Complex	50 mg	✓		✓
Vitamin C	500 mg chewable	✓		
Vitamin E plus selenium	E-400 IU with selenium 200 mcg	✓		
Mega or ultra multi-minerals	one capsule	✓		
Lecithin	1200 mg	✓		✓
Methionine	500 mg	✓		
Carnitine	250 mg	✓		
Milk thistle	250 mg or Liquid (1 ml)	✓		
Goldenseal root and echinacea mix	Liquid (1 ml) on weekend mornings	✓		
Water	Use water chart to calculate Part A & B	_____oz. from Part A		_____oz. from Part B

*   Take anytime *before* drinking, preferably with food. You may also take them all at once, however, these amounts are more efficiently absorbed when spread out over time. If your schedule only permits taking them at one time do so.

Sub-level IIa

Sub-level IIa can be used any 14 days out of each month	Amount	*Take anytime before drinking (Example)	Record the time that you will take the life-force nutrient	Take again within 2 hours after your last drink
B-complex	50 mg	breakfast		✓
Vitamin C	500 mg	breakfast		
Mega or ultra multi-minerals	one capsule	lunch		✓
Vitamin E plus selenium	E-400 IU with selenium 200 mcg	breakfast		
Lecithin	1200 mg	breakfast		✓
Dandelion	250 mg or 1 ml liquid	breakfast		
Water	Use water chart to calculate Part A & B	_____oz. from Part A		_____oz. from Part B

* Take at any meal. Avoid taking minerals when consuming coffee, tea, or high fiber cereal.

Level II   Life-Force Nutrient Monthly Rotation

	Sun	Mon	Tues	Wed	Thur	Fri	Sat
Week 1	Level IIa	Level II	Level II	Level II	Level II	Level II	Level II
Week 2	Level IIa	Level IIa	Level IIa	Level II	Level IIa	Level IIa	Level IIa
Week 3	Level IIa	Level IIa	Level IIa	Level II	Level IIa	Level IIa	Level IIa
Week 4	Level IIa	Level II	Level II	Level II	Level II	Level II	Level II

Level III   Life-Force Nutrient Protection

Life-force nutrients required when drinking 10 or more drinks	Amount	*Take anytime before drinking	Record the time that you will take the life-force nutrient	Take again anytime during drinking	Take again within 2 hours after your last drink
B-Complex	50 mg	✓		✓	✓
Vitamin C	500 mg chewable	✓		✓	
Vitamin E plus selenium	E-400 IU with 200 mg selenium	✓			✓
Mega or ultra multi-minerals	one capsule	✓			
Lecithin	1200 mg	✓			✓
Carnitine	250 mg	✓			✓
Glutathione	50 mg			✓	
Methionine	500 mg			✓	
Goldenseal root and echinacea mix	liquid (1 ml)	on weekend mornings			
Milk thistle	250 mg	✓			
Dandelion	475 mg	three days a week			
Water	use water chart to calculate Part A & B	_____oz. from Part A			_____oz. from Part B

* Take at any meal. Avoid taking minerals when consuming coffee, tea, or high fiber cereal.

Sub-level IIIa

Sub-level IIIa can be used any 14 days out of each month	Amount	*Take anytime before drinking (Example)	Record the time that you will take the life-force nutrient	Take again anytime during drinking	Take again within 2 hours after your last drink
B-complex	50 mg	breakfast		✓	✓
Vitamin E plus selenium	E-400 IU with selenium 200 mg	breakfast			✓
Mega or ultra multi-minerals	one capsule	lunch			
Milk thistle	250 mg	breakfast			✓
Artichoke, milk thistle, and dandelion blend	475 mg	three days a week			
Methio-nine	500 mg	right before drinking is best			✓
Carnitine	250 mg	right before drinking is best			
Vitamin C	500 mg	1-breakfast 1-dinner		✓	
Water	use water chart to calculate Part A & B	_____oz. from Part A			_____oz. from Part B

* Take at any meal, avoid taking minerals when consuming coffee, tea, or high fiber cereal.

Level III   Life-Force Nutrient Monthly Rotation

	Sun	Mon	Tues	Wed	Thur	Fri	Sat
Week 1	Level IIIa	Level III	Level III	Level III	Level III	Level III	Level III
Week 2	Level IIIa	Level IIIa	Level IIIa	Level III	Level IIIa	Level IIIa	Level IIIa
Week 3	Level IIIa	Level IIIa	Level IIIa	Level III	Level IIIa	Level IIIa	Level IIIa
Week 4	Level IIIa	Level III	Level III	Level III	Level III	Level III	Level III

A Word About Monthly Cycles

I find it easier to highlight the sub-level days on a calendar that hangs on my kitchen wall. Then at a glance I know which level to follow for any particular day. If you know certain days of the month are very hectic for you, schedule up to fourteen days as sub-level days. You may also decide to use sub-level days when you go on vacation since it minimizes the number of supplements you must pack. Some drinkers will alternate each day of the week between their level and sub-level. The critical point to remember is at least fourteen days per month should be at the regular level. The weeks or days you choose is up to you.

Drinking healthier in terms of the number of "pills" taken per day is similar to the amount consumed by elite athletes to gain a competitive edge. Many "gym" enthusiasts also take a similar amount of supplements. Why? Because they know their diet does not provide the nutrients required to heal and grow their muscles. Remember, drinking is a workout for your liver. Moreover, every cell damaged by alcohol needs to be replaced or repaired.

When a coach tells an athlete to take energy or protein supplements to perform at a higher level, the athlete follows the advice to the letter. Drinking healthier is no different. If you want to minimize free-radical damage, premature aging, organ dysfunction, and colds and infections from lowered immunity, you must follow the level that corresponds with the amount you drink.

Case Study

Kathy was a 32-year-old graphic artist who came from a family of heavy drinkers. She knew firsthand the medical problems life-long drinkers develop. She too was a heavy drinker, but did not want to head down the path of declining health. She also did not want to stop drinking. At 5'3" and 150 pounds, Kathy was overweight and had high blood pressure. Kathy also had a weak immune system and was frequently missing work due to flu-like symptoms. Her food intake consisted of a pastry and coffee at breakfast, burger and fries at lunch, and a frozen dinner after work.

She never took vitamins and neither did any of her family members. Kathy looked much older than her age, people often thought she was at least 40. The years of unprotected drinking allowed free radicals to attack her skin and rob it of its elasticity. Her eyes lacked brightness and her skin was dull and dehydrated. I instructed Kathy to follow sub-level IIa contained in this chapter and the information on "base-level" calories. After one year, Kathy improved the condition of her skin, lost 20 pounds, lowered her blood pressure, and increased her energy level. Kathy has shared her knowledge with her family and reported that drinking healthier has become a family affair.

Commonly Asked Questions About Supplements

Question: I am too tired to remember to take my life-force nutrients after drinking. What should I do?

Answer: Plan ahead and have your nutrients placed on a napkin next to your bed or near your toothbrush. Have a glass of water ready and swallow them down before going to bed. Pretend it's one last drink! If you are required to take nutrients during drinking, you must remember to bring them along, unless you are drinking at home. The easiest way is to put them in your pocket, purse, or plastic pill carrier. Develop a habit of setting out your life-force nutrients ahead of time. This way they can be easily taken. Try portioning a day's supply of life-force nutrients into a baggie the night before. Then in the morning you can grab the baggie and go. Purchase a pocket-sized pill holder for travel or when you will be away from home while drinking. As a last resort you can wrap them in a tissue. However, if you forget to take the pills they can end up in the wash. I have ruined many a good shirt while using the tissue method.

Question: Are the multi-mineral capsules listed under each of the 3 levels of life-force nutrient supplementation the same as a multi-vitamin?

Answer: No. Multi-mineral capsules contain only minerals. There are no vitamins in a multi-mineral capsule. If you want to take a multi-vitamin I would suggest Centrum or the generic equivalent. You do not need a heavy duty multi-vitamin since you are taking all the other life-force nutrients.

Question: Does one ultra or mega multi-mineral contain 100% of the RDAs?

Answer: It depends on the brand. Most require 3 capsules to meet 100 percent of the RDA. If you feel your diet is unbalanced take more than one capsule, but do not exceed the suggested mineral dosage set by the manufacturer. Many drinkers are not getting enough minerals from their food and may need to take an extra multi-mineral.

Question: Should I buy capsules or tablets?

Answer: It depends on what nutrient you are buying. When you buy the multi-mineral mentioned above, it's best if you purchase the capsule form. Be sure you see the word "chelated" or "amino acid chelated," which refers to a process that improves the mineral's absorption. Mineral tablets and non-chelated minerals are difficult to absorb. Both are cheaper not only in cost but quality too. When you buy glutathione, carnitine, and methionine you can buy either tablet or capsule since the tablets break down fairly well in most people.

    However, if you want to be absolutely certain you are absorbing what you are paying for, buy capsules. Vitamin E and lecithin are available in gel capsules and break down easily. If you have difficulty absorbing fat or desire to take vitamin E with your B-complex, buy the vitamin E in water soluble form. Chewable tablets are absorbed well and taste great too. Remember to rinse your mouth after chewing vitamin C because the acid damages your tooth enamel.

Question: You mentioned that tablets are difficult to absorb, but how can I tell?

Answer: There are a couple of home methods to determine if the tablet will break down in your body. Drop the tablet in a glass of water and see if it falls apart within fifteen to twenty minutes. Drop another tablet in a cup of vinegar and wait fifteen minutes. If the tablet crumbles in water and vinegar the odds are good your body will be able to absorb it. If it does not crumble in both solutions do not use it!

    The other method is to keep a plastic knife handy in the bathroom and after evacuating your colon, splice the stool lengthwise and then into quarters. When tablets do not dissolve in the small intestines they exit the body in whole or partial form and can be easily identified in your stool. I stress the importance of using a plastic knife rather than your good silver! Splicing your stool is like being a researcher for a few moments and can really help determine if you are just flushing away your hard earned dollar.

Question: Are there any nutrients a drinker should avoid taking too much of?

Answer: Yes, iron and beta-carotene. That is why I did not list them as nutrients to supplement heavily. Alcohol increases iron absorption. If the drinker takes a separate iron tablet, too much iron will be stored in the liver and cause damage. The amount found in the multi-mineral capsule would not be too much since it takes between three and six capsules to obtain 100 percent of the RDA.

A drinker should not take any additional iron without consulting her physician. Beta-carotene should not be taken right before, during, or immediately after drinking since the MEOS system of alcohol processing can convert beta-carotene into a toxic substance. The best time to take beta-carotene is the morning after drinking when alcohol is no longer present. This is very important to remember.

Question: Can I take the life-force nutrients on an empty stomach?

Answer: Yes. However, many people prefer to take their supplements with food to avoid belching up the taste of the vitamins later in the day. It's your choice. The important thing is to swallow the capsules with plenty of liquids. This will ensure they are pushed into the stomach and do not stick in your food pipe.

Question: How come when I take vitamins my urine comes out bright yellow or greenish yellow?

Answer: This means your cells are now saturated with vitamins and cannot hold any more. This is good. You never want to have urine come out clear or brownish. Brown colored urine may mean kidney trouble or lack of water intake. Clear as spring water means your body is running low or is already empty of life-force nutrients.

Question: My mouth has a funny awful taste the morning after drinking. Why?

Answer: Did you brush and floss before you went to bed? Even if you did brush, your mouth pores are trying to clean themselves of alcohol's presence from the night before. Moreover, your lungs excrete small quantities of alcohol which exit as vapor via your nose and mouth. During sleep, a warm closed mouth is a playground for bacteria which may feed on alcohol remnants, producing foul odors during the process.

The best way to improve the taste of your mouth is to brush your teeth and tongue prior to bed; in the morning scrape your tongue with a spoon, and rinse your mouth until the water looks clear as it goes down the drain. This will remove bacteria, alcohol residues, and dead taste-bud cells from your mouth.

Question: Can I use liquid B-complex?

Answer: Yes, just make sure you take enough to provide the amount specified in your level. Most herbs come in a liquid or capsule form too. The liquid form is probably better absorbed. Try both and decide which is more pleasant.

Question: I understand which life-force nutrients I need to take and when to take them, but should I eat or avoid certain foods when I drink?

Answer: Yes, and that is the topic of the next chapter.

Before, During, and After Drinking: Foods to Eat and Avoid

What contemptible scoundrel stole the cork from my lunch? — W.C. Fields

Before I learned to drink healthier I followed the drinking advice of my elders. Their voices echoed in my brain, "You better eat something before you drink if you want to keep your head and prevent getting sick." With this in mind I would eat a big greasy burger or fried chicken dinner before heading out for a night of power drinking, only to return home bloated and ready for a session of projectile vomiting. The idea of eating before and during drinking appeared to be sound advice. So why did I feel so bad afterwards? Because heavy drinking and eating do not mix well together. Period.

There are so many myths concerning how to drink that it's not surprising so many people feel lousy after a night of drinking. A small minority of drinkers have an iron stomach and can eat anything they choose whenever they want. The rest of us are not so lucky. One thing is for certain; the more you eat before, during, and after drinking the greater your chances of feeling sick and getting a hangover.

Drinking Myths of Majestic Proportions

- Liquor "shots" will get you drunk faster than beer, wine, or mixed drinks
- Drinking on an empty stomach will make you sick
- Drinking on an empty stomach will give you an ulcer
- Eating before and during drinking enables you to tolerate alcohol better
- Milk coats your stomach and enables you to drink more without getting sick
- Bread absorbs alcohol like a sponge, preventing stomach upset while drinking
- If you are drinking beer, never switch to wine or spirits; it will make you sick
- If you are drinking wine or spirits, never switch to beer; it will make you sick
- Drinking different cocktails in one night will make you sick
- Never eat raw shellfish while drinking liquor; stones will form and make you sick
- Alcohol is fattening
- Vodka is the purest and least likely spirit to cause a hangover
- Drinking the dog that bit you cures a hangover
- Coffee will sober you up
- You can "walk off" the alcohol

More worrisome, eating during or after drinking can cause obesity and a fatty liver condition. It's unfortunate that hangovers are the most memorable experience people have after they drink. They follow all the myths and still end up kneeling before the toilet, and like many drinkers they are unaware they can break this viscious hangover cycle. I often wonder if this was the intention of the original "framers" of the drinking myths that still circulate today. Did a group of anti-drinking fanatics get together years ago to devise drinking myths with the intention of making drinking a truly negative experience? I guess they figured drinking might turn out to be too much fun and that would be bad for society. It appears so, because everything I discovered about how to drink healthier is the complete opposite of what I had been told.

Alcohol is Alcohol: There is No Difference

Many drinkers are hesitant to switch from one drink to another. They believe certain drink combinations will make them sick. This is simply not true. Alcohol is alcohol, no matter what label is on the bottle. The chemical structure of ethanol, or alcohol as it is better known, is $CH_3\ CH_2\ OH$ whether you drink beer, wine, spirits, sangria, coolers, champagne, or cactus squeezings.

All forms of alcohol are equal in the eyes of the liver, which sees alcohol solely as a chemical structure. The important thing is to choose drinks that appeal to your taste, and eat only those foods that marry well with alcohol. However, if you firmly believe mixing alcohol will make you sick, it probably will. The mind is a powerful thing and it can turn simple thought into reality. Many people will themselves to be successful. They visualize success and do a significant amount of self-talk, and success comes.

Likewise, if you witness a drinker vomit and overhear his friend say, "I told you to stick with beer," your brain will register this event. As this belief is reinforced by similar events, the negative association between mixing drinks and sickness becomes a self-fulfilling prophecy each time you mix. It's a simple case of mind over matter. Therefore, from this day forward, believe that alcohol is alcohol and enjoy a variety of drinks without the worry of impending sickness.

The Hangover: An Interaction of Food and Alcohol

Alcohol, fruit juices, and finely chewed carbohydrates empty quickly from the stomach. Why? Because these items do not require digestion by the stomach. Protein foods are held in the stomach longer because protein digestion occurs there. Due to their viscosity and aversion to water, fats naturally delay the stomach from emptying even though no significant fat digestion takes place there. When fat finally empties into the intestines it can still signal the stomach to delay further emptying.

However, when carbohydrate, protein, fat, and alcohol are consumed together, the stomach delays the whole mixture from being emptied. The extra time in the stomach causes the fruit and vegetable sugars, yeast products, and refined flours to "stew" in a "brew" of alcohol and stomach acid. This interaction is negative, resulting in the formation of putrid material. When the stomach starts to release this material into the intestines, it can be rejected, causing the drinker to vomit. Moreover, this is precisely why drinker's vomit smells so terrible!

Many drinkers do not vomit, and the putrid material is released into the intestines. There it is further degraded and fermented by bacteria before being absorbed into the body. The absorbed mixture creates an allergic-like process that results in a hangover. Cellular water loss from brain cells and lack of life-force nutrients compound this discomfort, and the drinker mistakenly blames alcohol for his or her misery.

The more you drink, the more you need to be concerned about which foods you select and how well you chew. If you only drink a couple of glasses of wine with dinner, it probably does not matter what you ate before dinner, or which foods you choose at dinner. If two drinks with dinner cause you to feel bloated and uncomfortable or have a hangover, you should allow your food to digest for three to five hours before having a drink. The bloating may have been due to fat from an earlier meal signaling your stomach to delay emptying. If you plan to have more than two drinks with dinner or continue drinking afterwards, you should pay close attention to what you eat before, during, and after drinking. It can make a world of difference in how you feel in the morning.

It takes the same amount of time to eat the right foods as it does the wrong foods. Doesn't it make sense to avoid those foods that are incompatible with drinking, and in doing so minimize the chances of a hangover?

How to Prevent a Hangover

In order to prevent a hangover and maintain good health, drinking must be treated like an organized activity. There must be some general rules to guide drinkers safely through the event. There is a right way and a wrong way to perform any activity, or at the very least there is a best way. If you perform an exercise without instruction it can result in injury and pain.

Likewise, haphazard drinking results in the dreaded hangover. Believe me when I say there is a pain-free way to drink.

Personally, I do not enjoy the agony of a hangover and neither do you. Based on the faulty premise that drinking on an empty stomach will make them sick, many people decide to eat before and during drinking. Most people make poor food choices and experience discomfort afterwards. Let's face it. Most people cannot make nutritious food choices when they are stone sober. What type of judgment do you think is exercised after two or three drinks? How about after eight?

At one time or another we have all surrendered to the temptation of eating during or after drinking. As the ruling faculties of the mind go under conscious sedation, food becomes very appealing. We overeat the wrong foods, often with disastrous results in terms of next-day productivity. The foods you eat before, during, and after drinking greatly determine how well you will feel the next day. Because alcohol receives top priority handling, certain foods end up fermenting or rotting in your stomach while waiting their turn to be processed. When you drink, avoid foods that require longer digestion times and decompose in the presence of alcohol. Always finely chew your food if you are drinking with meals or will be drinking later. Large pieces of food increase stomach acid and delay the stomach from emptying, which increases the risk of vomiting and hangover. Avoid milk if you will be drinking. It increases stomach acid and forms a hard curd that can make a drinker ill. The following beverages are in the order of increasing acid production: water < cola < decaffeinated coffee < 7-up <tea < coffee < beer < milk. If you often have an acid stomach, cut back on the amount of milk, beer, and coffee you drink. Another beverage that produces a significant amount of acid is red wine. Try white wine if the reds cause you grief. Remember, alcohol does not require digestion and extra stomach acid only causes the body to work harder.

The Rules of Pain Free Drinking

- Always remember to take the right level of life-force nutrients
- Choose from the Best-foods list and avoid the Worst-foods list
- Allow *three hours* after your last meal of Best foods *before* starting to drink
- If you eat from the list of Worst foods allow *five hours before* drinking
- Refrain from eating foods on the Worst list during or after drinking
- Drink the amount of water from Part A and B of the water chart
- Drink 8 oz. of warm lemon-honey water prior to sleep and after you rise to urinate
- The more you drink the less you should eat during and after drinking
- You can eat more only if you plan to drink less
- You cannot both drink and eat heavily and expect to stay healthy and hangover free
- Always know how much you can safely drink
- Finely chew your food and you will reduce the risk of vomiting and hangover
- Do not drink coffee or tea after drinking
- To avoid a hangover choose the best foods after drinking
- To avoid obesity choose mainly from the Best-foods list
- The morning after drinking eat eggs and salsa or hot cereal and one B-complex vitamin

At the end of this chapter, I provide you with a list of the worst and best foods to eat before, during, and after drinking. The best-foods list contains base or alkaline-forming foods and those that marry well with alcohol. Ever wonder why Alka-Seltzer or baking soda work so well at relieving the discomfort of hangovers and indigestion? It's because they are alkaline. The worst-foods list contains acid-forming foods, yeast, fat, insoluble protein, and food items susceptible to decomposing in alcohol.

Never Perform Strenuous Activities on a Full Stomach

Eat a full meal and then try to run your fastest mile. Think you could do it? Probably not. At the very least your performance will suffer, and at worst you will be belching or puking. Why? Because digestion and absorption of food causes a huge shift of blood flow into the intestines. The extra blood is necessary to perform the work of digestion. Where does the blood come from? The arms, legs, and upper torso which then have to function on less blood and oxygen, causing poor muscle performance throughout the body. Digestion increases the number of breaths you take per minute, decreasing your oxygen and the ability to run, perform other work, or process alcohol.

Liquids and finely chewed carbohydrates always empty faster from an empty stomach. Witness the effectiveness of sports drinks that contain substantial carbohydrates. They are formulated to quickly exit the stomach and get into the body without shifting blood into the intestines and away from the muscles. Therefore, eating a heavy meal full of fat, protein, and carbohydrates creates competition for blood between the digestive and the muscle systems, and the muscles lose every time. The whole body pays for this mistake, the muscles cramp and tire quickly, the stomach aches as muscles try to draw blood back in their direction, and you may vomit or feel nauseous.

Drinking is a strenuous activity, too. Similar problems occur when the gastrointestinal system is processing a heavy load of food, and alcohol starts showing up at the scene. Whereas exercising muscle tries to pull blood away from the digestive system, alcohol makes the whole system slow down. Alcohol diverts the attention of the digestive system away from the food and towards processing alcohol first. This creates a state of stagnation which can give rise to similar symptoms as those encountered while running on a full stomach. Moreover, imagine an enzyme hungry and willing to neutralize alcohol having to wade through your pork dinner with all the trimmings in order to find the alcohol! This makes a compelling argument for drinking on an empty stomach.

To Drink or Not to Drink on an Empty Stomach: That is the Question!

Drinking on a full stomach never worked for me. I usually felt bloated while drinking and sick the next morning. All I wanted from drinking was a clarity of mind that only alcohol can gently usher in. No longer a prisoner of the status quo, I decided to perform drinking experiments using my body as a laboratory. I reduced my food intake before drinking and avoided acid-forming foods and chose mostly base-forming and easily digested foods. This immediately improved my tolerance for alcohol and minimized much of the dreaded hangover. I then progressed to drinking on an empty stomach. I discovered that drinking on an empty stomach allowed me to reach my state of mind in the fewest number of drinks. All-in-all it worked! This led me to embark upon what would become a lifelong practice of drinking on an empty stomach. I have never developed an ulcer, nor have I experienced a real hangover since I started avoiding certain foods before, during, and after drinking.

Drinking on an empty stomach allows faster neutralization of alcohol, especially if you drink hard liquor. Higher concentrations of alcohol activate the stomach's neutralizing enzymes that catch alcohol before it sneaks under the stomach lining, and heads for the brain. Food dilutes the concentration of alcohol to a level that does not adequately stimulate these enzymes. Therefore, if you eat right before or during drinking it only serves to slow the rate and not the amount of alcohol to the brain. Drinking on an empty stomach may initially cause alcohol to travel to the brain faster, but the overall amount will be less because more of the alcohol will be neutralized. I believe this is the difference between having a hangover and having a good morning.

It is worth mentioning that beer, wine, and diluted mixed drinks taken on an empty stomach do not activate neutralizing enzymes in the same fashion as straight liquor. The higher alcohol content of straight liquor stimulates the body to neutralize it at a faster rate. When it comes to drinking, beverage temperature is important. Cold alcohol beverages stay in the stomach longer than those at room temperature. This is especially important if you drink alcohol with meals. Cold beer or iced alcohol drinks increase the likelihood of stomach upset. A double whammy in terms of delaying the stomach from emptying occurs when cold beer or iced drinks are consumed in a cold environment. Straight liquor at room temperature is emptied from the stomach and neutralized faster than cold beer, wine, or mixed drinks. However, wine is the best form of alcohol to have with meals.

Most people choose alcohol to enjoy the feeling that comes with gentle indulgence. Otherwise, they would choose cheaper non-alcohol beverages. Food slows the rate of alcohol absorption, causing many drinkers to have a second or third drink. The additional drinks are necessary to achieve the lost "euphoria" that should have been provided by the first drink if it had been consumed on an empty stomach. Therefore, a belly full of food may cause more drinking, not less, and stimulates the decomposition process described earlier. I really believe if drinkers knew that the chances of getting sick decrease when drinking on an empty stomach, they would opt to drink less and feel better. Every drinker should know his or her upper drinking limit, the point at which an additional drink provides no additional benefits. This should not be a fuzzy number. You should know precisely how much you can drink safely under all conditions. Moreover, you should never exceed this amount in a new environment. If you have never consumed more than four shots of tequila, don't try for number five at the office party or your favorite nightclub. If you must develop your drinking prowess, it should always be done at home where you can safely monitor the effect of the extra drink. This is very important. Drinking is not a game. The 21st Century Drinker does not participate in drinking contests. The only thing she has to prove is that she can drink healthier. The act of drinking should be the aftermath of sound self-research and nothing less.

I laugh silently to myself when someone tells me to drink a certain way, or to eat this or that before and during drinking. I know precisely how alcohol affects me from one drink to the next. I start my drinking three hours after my last meal of best foods, I never eat while drinking, and I choose from the best-foods list after drinking. I developed the food lists after years of research and believe all drinkers will benefit from them whenever they drink. Certainly, there are times when I indulge in the worst-foods list, but I always feel better when I avoid them.

I know exactly how one glass of wine on an empty stomach makes me feel, and so should you. Likewise, I know how each successive drink will lead me down the familiar road that leads to my plateau, a state where I am in balance with thought and universe. Two drinks beyond this point my marginal utility for one more drink turns negative, meaning it detracts from all the good acquired during the first eight or so drinks. It's like this symbol ∩; the left side is productive drinking that plateaus at the peak and then rapidly declines with continued drinking. All drinkers should know, understand, and practice this concept. I have taken all the guesswork and chance out of my drinking, distilling it into a science, and you must learn to do this, too.

I wholeheartedly recommend that you pick an afternoon or evening in which you are free of any responsibility that requires total judgment. Then purchase your favorite alcohol beverage, curl up with a video or loved one, or both, and let the drinking begin. This will teach you an important lesson about the effects of alcohol on an empty stomach. When I say an empty stomach I mean your last meal should have been at least three hours ago, and preferably from the best-foods list. You will be surprised. It's not scary, you will not start to babble or speak in tongues, and most important of all, you will not become sick or develop a fatty liver or waist.

Then the next time you're in a social setting you will not feel compelled to belly up to the buffet or hors d'oeuvres table with the false illusion that food is a drinker's friend. Instead you can confidently drink on an empty stomach with full knowledge that you can handle it.

A 21st Century Drinker knows alcohol's raw effect, having experienced its unadulterated form free of disturbing food. If someone offers you another drink before you are ready just say, "No thank you, not right now. I enjoyed the first on an empty stomach and it's still performing marvelously." This is the ultimate 21st Century Drinker's response that will surely get the party conversation flowing.

If you are going to have more than a few drinks, and your goal is to enjoy the presence of alcohol and feel normal in the morning, drinking on an empty stomach can lead you to your goal.

The Benefits of Drinking on an Empty Stomach

- Quickly activates alcohol processing and neutralization
- Prevents fat gain
- Minimizes the chances of vomiting and hangover
- Reduces restlessness, allowing sound sleep
- Eliminates belching and the bloated feeling
- Allows prior food intake to be properly digested and absorbed without mutation
- Low calorie inexpensive fun that can be enjoyed alone or as part of a group
- Prevents indigestion and the need for antacids
- Eliminates the need for aspirin, Tylenol, Alka-Seltzer or Pepto-Bismol
- Eliminates food fermentation and the formation of allergenic substances

Drinking and Eating Timetable

Most people drink haphazardly, giving little thought to the timing of their food and drink. The idea that some foods mix better with alcohol while others mix poorly is given no consideration. Upon waking, your stomach is literally empty. Drinkers should not drink immediately in this condition. It is critical to their health that they consume some nourishing food and wait a few hours before they begin to drink.

If you want to start drinking at:	You should stop eating by:
10:00 a.m.	7:00 a.m.
1:00 p.m.	10:00 a.m.
4:00 p.m.	1:00 p.m.
7:00 p.m.	4:00 p.m.
9:00 p.m.	6:00 p.m.
10:00 p.m.	7:00 p.m.
11:00 p.m.	8:00 p.m.
After 11:00 p.m.	8:00 p.m.*

* If you work late day shifts and finish work after 11:00 p.m., eat your last meal 3 hours before your first drink.

Why Are These the Best Foods to Eat?

The foods listed below provide your blood with alkaline or base-forming foods that counteract the acid-forming nature of alcohol processing. Many diseases and illness stem from bacteria or viruses that thrive in an acid environment. Drinking can create such a home. These foods create an alkaline environment unsuitable for bacteria and sickness. When drinkers use antacids, baking soda, or Pepto-Bismol they obtain relief. By eating base forming foods you minimize the production of acid and can avoid needing these products.

Certain foods such as corn are high in methionine, which is an essential amino acid used as a building block for making chemicals that help detoxify the liver. Garlic has bacteria fighting capabilities, healing properties, and contains sulfur which is the active agent in methionine and vitamin B1. Each of the foods listed below support the common goal of drinking

healthier and are easily digested, and low in yeast, fat, and milk
protein.

The Best Foods to Eat *Before* Drinking

Vegetables Prepare steamed or lightly cooked, no added oil, margarine or butter	Ripened Fruits and Juices	Starch No added milk, margarine, butter, lard, or oil	Protein Grilled, steamed, broiled, pan fried in Teflon pan, or boiled. No added oil, margarine, butter or lard
Radishes	Fresh pineapple	Steamed Rice, with or without soy sauce	4 oz. any white fish
Artichokes Celery	Lemons	Oatmeal	4 oz. chicken or turkey breast
Tomatoes	Lime	Pasta	1-4 Eggs
Carrots	Apples	Potato with skin	4 oz. Shrimp
Lettuce	Blueberries	Unleavened bread	4 oz. Lobster
Cucumbers	Boysenberries	Whole grain crackers	4 oz. Crab meat
Eggplant	Strawberries	Cream of rice	Fresh tuna (or canned in water)
Okra	Raspberries		Whey protein
Green onion	Pears		
Garlic	Cherries		
Yellow dock	Oranges		
Parsley	Grapefruits		
Corn	Plums		
Beets	Grapes		

If fruits give you gas, take two capsules of Goldenseal root
and Echinacea prior to eating. Do not eat unripe fruit; it
contains too much indigestible starch.

The Best Foods to Eat *During* Drinking

Vegetables No dips, only salsa	Ripened Fruits and Juices	Starch No dips, only salsa	Protein Prepared as above
Radishes	Lemons	Whole grain crackers	White fish
Celery	Limes	Unleavened bread	Chicken breast
Tomatoes	Maraschino cherries	Pretzels	Turkey breast
Cucumbers	Oranges	Baked potato chips	Shrimp
Carrots	Pineapple	Baked corn chips	Lobster
Artichokes	Grapes	Corn Chex cereal	Crab meat
Beets	Cherries	Rice Chex cereal	Tuna
	Blueberries		
	Strawberries		
	Boysenberries		
	Raspberries		
	Melon		

* Remember, if you want to eat during drinking, you should want to take your life-force nutrients as well, if your drinking level requires this.

The Best Foods to Eat *After** Drinking

Beverage	Carbohydrate (choose one)	Protein (choose one)
Lemon water: juice from one fresh lemon mixed in 8 oz. water, flavor with 1 tsp. of honey	2 or 3 crackers with jelly or jam	2 oz. skinless chicken or turkey breast
	Small slice of fat free cake ½-1 cup nonfat ice cream	Cooked egg whites with strawberry jam, no added fat

* Remember, if you want to eat *after* drinking, you should want to take your life-force nutrients as well, if your drinking level requires this.

Why These are the Best Foods to Eat After Drinking

- Low fat foods: alcohol decreases the fat-burning ability of the liver
- Lemon: a liver stimulant, liquefies bile, nourishes nerves, and dissolves impurities
- Protein: heals and repairs cell damage, and transports fat from the liver during sleep
- Fructose: helps complete alcohol processing and minimizes hangovers

The Worst Foods to Eat
*Before, During, and After Drinking

Protein	Starches	Fats	Beverages
Salmon and other fatty fish	Fried rice, macaroni & cheese	Butter, margarine	Coffee, tea
Red meat	Banana	Vegetable oils	**Milk
All fried meats, any meat with added nitrites	All breads that are not made from whole grains	Lard Mayonnaise	
Sausages, salami, pepperoni type meats	Pancakes and waffles	Avocado	
Dark chicken or turkey meat, pizza	Anything deep-fat fried, onion rings, fries, potato skins, mozzarella sticks, breaded vegetables	White sauces Salad dressing Sour cream Cheese sauces Gravy	
Duck and goose	Mashed potatoes	Bacon	
Liver and other organ meats	Corn chips, potato chips	Nuts, peanut butter	
Cheese	Cheese puffs	Ice cream	
Yogurt	Cookies	Other high fat desserts	

* If you must eat these foods, consume them no later than 5 hours before your first drink. However, the best recommenda-

tion is avoid these foods entirely on heavy drinking days. *None of these foods should be consumed during or after drinking.*
** Milk protein forms a curd that delays the emptying of the stomach.

Why These Are the Worst Foods to Eat Before, During, and After Drinking

Because they:
- Increase the amount of acids
- Are difficult to digest
- Contain yeast
- Delay stomach emptying
- Form putrid substances in the presence of alcohol
- Are high in fat
- Cause fat gain and fatty liver.

Food for Thought

For many years I have monitored the interactions between alcohol and food. I performed countless experiments that required drinking on both an empty and full stomach. The lists of best and worst foods are the culmination of my efforts to provide all drinkers with a starting point. You may have a unique ability to tolerate other foods not mentioned; or you may be able to consume the worst foods no matter how much you drink. If so, you are a lucky drinker. However, all drinkers will discover that the best foods marry well with alcohol. Therefore, when you absolutely need to feel 100 percent productive in the morning, choose only those foods from the best lists.

The important point to remember is you should eat like royalty three to five hours before drinking; like a commoner during drinking; and like a pauper after drinking. Otherwise, you increase your risk of obesity, fatty liver, and hangover. Obesity is a risk factor for many diseases, one of which is heart disease. Heart attack and stroke are preventable conditions. Luckily for the drinker, alcohol plays a protective role in the battle against heart disease, which is the subject of the next chapter.

How Alcohol Can Protect You From a Heart Attack and Stroke

Wine nourishes, refreshes, and cheers... Whenever wine is lacking, medicines become necessary. — Talmud

The beauty of drinking healthier is the protection it offers every cell in your body, and not just those involved in alcohol processing. Drinking healthier reduces your overall risk of heart attack and stroke by supplying:

- Anti-oxidants
- Magnesium
- Potassium
- Vitamin B12
- Folate

- Base level calorie information to reduce abdominal obesity.

A number of research studies show that people who had heart attacks also had lower levels of magnesium, folate, and other life-force nutrients. They also displayed higher levels of a chemical called homocysteine, which may increase the risk of heart disease. Vitamin B12, and possibly folate, are needed to convert homocysteine into the "liver friendly" essential amino acid methionine. This conversion lowers the level of homocysteine in the blood. Alcoholics have higher levels of homocysteine, and lower levels of B6, B12, and folate. This is probably why some drinkers have heart attacks.

More importantly, heart attack victims tend to have higher amounts of oxidized cholesterol. This can be explained by their lower levels of anti-oxidants, which enable free radicals to damage or oxidize cholesterol. Remember, free radicals are looking for a partner, and cholesterol is one of their main targets. Oxidized cholesterol appears to be partly responsible for clogging arteries and blood vessels. Drinking healthier provides the life-force nutrients required to prevent cholesterol oxidation, and free-radical, vessel, and heart damage.

Clearly, a non-drinker could achieve all of the above and reduce the chances of heart attack and stroke too. However, the drinker has an advantage that the non-drinker doesn't. Alcohol! Alcohol alone protects the heart by increasing the level of good cholesterol and preventing blood clots from forming. The increased level of good cholesterol lowers the risk of heart attack, and the prevention of blood clots minimizes the risk of stroke.

How Does Alcohol Protect Against Heart Attack and Stroke?

Alcohol naturally increases the level of good cholesterol (HDL), which in turn lowers the bad cholesterol (LDL). HDL is a cholesterol scavenger that floats in the blood system searching for "bad" cholesterol. HDL binds "bad" cholesterol and transports it to the liver, where it mixes with bile and is excreted into the intestinal tract for elimination. This is how "good" cholesterol lowers the "bad" cholesterol and reduces the risk of heart attack.

Alcohol naturally reduces the stickiness of the blood cells and platelets, and dissolves or reduces the formation of blood clots. If a blood clot forms it can block the narrow vessels leading to the brain. When this occurs oxygen is unable to reach the brain cells and they begin to die. This event is called a stroke. Afterwards, the stroke victim often must undergo a lengthy rehabilitation process to learn to walk and talk again. Because of its ability to dissolve or prevent the formation of life threatening clots, alcohol is also nicknamed a "blood thinner."

Therefore, alcohol has medical merit in its ability to lower the risk of heart attack and stroke. Numerous research studies support these facts. One study showed that individuals with high levels of bad cholesterol benefited from alcohol the most. Another study revealed that inactive regular drinkers who stopped drinking for three weeks experienced a significant decline in good cholesterol. However, when they resumed drinking three drinks a day their good cholesterol shot back up significantly. A final study fed volunteers a regular diet and six drinks daily. This level of alcohol significantly increased the study participants' good cholesterol level.

Even with all this research there appears to be confusion as to how much alcohol is too much.

Current Recommendations Are Not Gospel

Alcohol protects our heart and vessels. This cannot be challenged. The question is, should we drink alcohol for medicinal purposes and if so, how much? Current recommendations in this country are two drinks per day for men and one for women. These recommendations overlook research that indicates that a range of two to seven drinks per day reduces heart attacks. I have no problem with people deciding on their own that two drinks is enough for them. However, they should not be told that drinking more than two drinks is counterproductive in terms of heart protection. I find it disturbing that our government and medical community scare us into believing two drinks is the "maximum" daily safe limit.

Why was the lower end of the range chosen instead of disclosing the full range? Because their agenda is to lower the per capita consumption of alcohol, not increase it, even though there is scant evidence that disclosing the range would cause a detrimental increase in drinking. Yes, careless unprotected drinking can cause a variety of health problems. However, a 21st Century Drinker can safely imbibe two to seven drinks per day and still be in the heart-healthy range. Clearly, the eighth drink does not cause heart damage; it just does not provide any additional heart benefits. I guess the heart understands the concept of marginal utility too!

Unfortunately, most people believe if they cross over the magical figure of "two drinks" they are headed down doom's road. This is simply not true. Studies have shown that drinkers who consume between two to seven drinks have a lower risk of heart disease. It does not mean these drinkers have the lowest risk of alcoholism, wife, husband, or child beating. (Although they could.) Likewise, this level of consumption does not make them more susceptible to becoming an alcoholic or acquiring the above abnormal behavior.

Why We Limit Ourselves to Two Drinks Per Day

We do this because we are part of an experiment called the "whole population theory." The powers that be sincerely believe they can influence the "problem" drinker by shifting downward the average per capita consumption of alcohol. The "population strategy" has been used for government recommendations on salt intake, fat intake, and other so called "harmful" desires which lurk in the hearts of all men and women. None of these population strategies have worked, and it will not work with alcohol. It is a desperate bureaucratic attempt to provide an easy solution to the very complex issue of "problem" drinking.

Campaigns that specify a limit on alcohol are intended to whittle away at the "problem" drinker and discourage others from becoming "problem" drinkers. This is a futile attempt that serves only to scare individuals who do not have a problem with alcohol. However, if moderate drinkers lower their consumption from four drinks a day to two, per capita consumption declines. Then the bureaucrats can claim that their campaign has reduced per capita alcohol consumption, and in doing so made our world safer, healthier, and more productive, even though in reality the decrease came primarily from those who drink the least. Meanwhile, the problem drinker continues to drink his or her usual amount. Does this make sense? Of course not. Overall consumption decreased, but the strategy fails because no one's risk profile was altered in a positive direction.

We should now be in agreement that the two drink "maximum" is an outgrowth of societal reliance on the "population strategy" as a way of addressing "problem" drinking. Furthermore, coercing moderate drinkers into limiting themselves to two drinks per day will never influence the "problem" drinkers to follow suit. Finally, 21st Century Drinkers base their consumption on their age, muscle mass, overall health, life-force nutrient stores, and tolerance level. Therefore, they should not accept the two-drink maximum as gospel. I think it's high time government health officials and the medical community start treating the citizenry as adults who can make their own decisions. Or at the very least they should explain the true intent of their national health recommendations.

Would the "True Range" Cause a Non-drinker or Occasional Drinker to Start Drinking More?

Exposing the true range of two to seven drinks will reduce the badgering that harmless drinkers experience. Too often I hear a well meaning friend or loved one tell a drinker to stop at two drinks. Why? Because that is the "safe" range. The drinker is told this even though he does not have a problem with alcohol, nor will he be driving afterwards. People often say to me, "Don't you worry that alcohol is bad for you or it may cause you to become an alcoholic?" Quite frankly I do not, and that is why I wrote this book. Those questions reveal to me that many people are afraid of alcohol. I know it's not fair; they simply do not know about drinking healthier. Nobody has ever sat them down and explained that they can protect their health while drinking. Drinkers and their loved ones deserve this peace of mind. Two drinks might be a safe upper limit to protect society from drunk drivers, but it is not the safe upper limit to protect you from a heart attack or stroke.

Studies have shown that non-drinkers have a greater risk of a heart attack when compared to drinkers. Does this mean all non-drinkers should start drinking? Of course not! If drinking has ruined your career or family relationships you should not drink. Period. However, if you do not have a problem with alcohol, and currently enjoy alcohol only on special occasions, you should consider the research.

I recommend that non-drinkers and occasional drinkers with low levels of good cholesterol start drinking moderately. This is defined as two to seven drinks daily. Clearly, I suggest starting out with one or two and over time evaluate your need for more. However, with equal enthusiasm I always recommend exercise and weight loss if needed. Alcohol is not a cure-all for heart attack; it is simply one of our weapons against it. Clearly, if you are obese, inactive, hypertensive, and lacking life-force nutrients, drinking will not protect you from the fate that awaits you.

People who disagree with my recommendation have a distorted view of the occasional drinker and non-drinker. These people believe the occasional drinker and non-drinker will fall hopelessly in love with drinking, and abandon responsibilities and become a "problem" drinker. This is absurd and insulting to all occasional drinkers and non-drinkers. An analogy will support my point.

I describe individuals who do not speed while driving as "non-speeders." Why does a non-speeder choose to stay within the set speed zones? Why not fall hopelessly in love with the thrill of speeding? Is it because the car cannot exceed the speed limit, and therefore they are non-speeders due to mechanical limitations? Hardly. Most cars on the road today can easily and safely exceed 100 miles per hour. Is it because he does not find speeding to be a thrill? Maybe. Could it be he has received too many tickets or is afraid of receiving his first? Could be. Aside from this last group, why are non-speeders not partaking in the act of rampant speeding on all roads and highways across America? Because he is exercising what he considers to be good judgment for his particular way of life. He has decided the risk versus the reward of traveling above the speed limit is unacceptable.

Clearly, many people speed safely, and others speed recklessly. Should we require all cars to have a maximum speed of 55 or 65 miles per hour? No, that would be inefficient and potentially dangerous because there are times when a driver must speed ahead to flee from danger. There is a time and place for speeding. Likewise, there is a time and place to allow yourself to drink, and that time comes when research enlightens you, or your doctor mentions that your HDLs are too low. Remember, your chances of dying from a heart attack or stroke are significantly greater than the threat of developing an alcohol-related health problem while drinking healthier.

If the medical community started recommending a range of two to seven drinks per day, every anti-drinking lobbying group across America would be against it. It's not that they are against the idea of heart protection, it's the idea of using alcohol as the method. They would worry that more people would drink and drive, commit crimes, and otherwise be negligent. Again, this is unfounded.

How Much Alcohol is Enough
to Protect the Heart?

Where do we draw the line between maximum heart benefit and the starting point of liver problems? Medical research indicates that cirrhosis of the liver on average develops after decades of drinking 13 or more drinks each day. Therefore, based on present research and my own experience counseling drinkers, I believe a 21st Century Drinker concerned about the risk of heart attack can safely enjoy up to seven drinks a day. Of course they could obtain a similar level of protection with less than seven drinks, although some research appears to indicate that drinkers who consume six to seven drinks have not only a lower risk of heart attack, but the *lowest* risk of heart attack.

If you're an occasional drinker who enjoys a drink or two now and then, consider having one or two each day. If you are a non-drinker because you were told alcohol is bad for you, consider the research and draw your own conclusion. If you are a regular drinker, draw comfort from the fact that the first seven drinks are heart healthy. The eighth drink and beyond offer no additional heart protection. Anyone who tells you that two drinks per day is the maximum in terms of heart protection is misinformed. If she continues to say seven drinks a day will cause other health problems, nod in agreement for she must be talking about *drinkers who do not know how to drink healthier.*

Heart Benefits of Drinking Healthier

> ♥ Anti-oxidants prevent LDL from being oxidized. Oxidized LDL causes clogged arteries and vessels resulting in heart attack and stroke
>
> ♥ Anti-oxidants protect cell membranes in the heart, brain, and lungs. Free radical damage is a seed that grows into a heart attack
>
> ♥ Alcohol increases good cholesterol which in turn helps to lower bad cholesterol
>
> ♥ Alcohol prevents the formation of life threatening clots

The Truth About Dietary Cholesterol: It Does Not Increase Your Risk of Heart Disease

A well known cholesterol researcher, Dr. Ancel Keys, was interviewed in *Eating Well* magazine (March/April 1997). His comment on the relationship between cholesterol and heart disease was, "...there's no connection whatsoever between cholesterol in food and cholesterol in the blood. None. And we've known that all along."

Amazing? Not really. Cholesterol in your blood is not from the food you eat. Your liver makes cholesterol every minute of the day to form healthy cell membranes, bile salts, vitamin D, and the sex hormones, testosterone and estrogen. Cholesterol is so important to your well-being that the body equipped itself with the ability to make its own supply. So how come most people view cholesterol as a villain? I could answer this with another question, "Why do people think it's bad to mix different types of alcohol?" Because they are misinformed. For decades the poor egg has been vilified as the cause of all heart attacks.

Case Study

Ed, a 34-year-old manager had a significant family history of heart disease. His grandfathers both died of a heart attack. One died at the age of 37, the other at 57. His father was currently being treated for a heart condition. This history prompted his physician to order a cholesterol test. The test revealed that Ed's good cholesterol (HDL) was only 27mg/dl. The normal level for a male is >45 mg/dl. His bad cholesterol (LDL) was 170 mg/dl. The normal range for LDL is 60-180 mg/dl. Ed had good reason to be concerned, and that is why he contacted me to help him improve his HDL level and overall cardiac risk profile.

Ed drank on average three to four drinks a month. He enjoyed drinking, but felt awful the next day when he awoke with a hangover. Moreover, he was under the impression that alcohol caused weight gain. At 5'10" and 225 pounds, Ed was not exactly a poster boy for health and fitness. Ed had heard that drinking could increase his HDL level and wanted guidance on developing a nutritional program that included alcohol for that purpose. Since Ed enjoyed wine I instructed him to start drinking two to three glasses of Chardonnay each night. He also started consuming life-force nutrients daily and drinking the prescribed amounts of water and protein his body needed. Six months later when his doctor repeated his blood work, Ed's LDL had decreased to 130mg/dl and his HDL increased to 38 mg/dl. A 25-pound weight loss and improved cholesterol profile was a direct result of healthier drinking. Any medical professional would agree that Ed reduced his risk of heart attack many-fold.

Many physicians and dietitians still do not understand that dietary cholesterol has no effect on blood cholesterol. They still teach patients to reduce their egg consumption. Some inform their patients to avoid shellfish, shrimp, and lobster too. This is pure ignorance, but people respectfully try to adhere to these thoughtless recommendations. Why does the health profession wish to deprive us of alcohol and certain foods? The next time a doctor or dietitian tells you to restrict the number of eggs you eat, refer him to the *Eating Well* magazine article above or to the research listed in the bibliography. Better yet, ask him point blank why he continues to ignore current medical research?

Several times in my life I have consumed up to a dozen eggs a day for months at a time, and my cholesterol has never been over 165 mg/dl. However, I do exercise and drink healthier.

It's a Matter of Education

Drinkers and non-drinkers are not feeble-minded people who must be shielded from the fact that drinking can protect the heart. If properly informed, they would not interpret the information as a license to drink in an uncontrolled manner. I believe people would exercise the same caution in their decision to drink as they do their decision to drive safely. Drinkers and drivers both know the penalties. Speeders eventually receive a ticket, or worse, they crash, and problem drinkers will see their network of family, friends, and career unravel. Both weigh the risk versus the rewards of their actions and act accordingly. Let's take a brave step forward and teach the nation about alcohol and how to drink healthier. This is an area that needs immediate educational resources, and not another "just say no" moron program so readily implemented by well meaning bureaucrats.

You now have the complete information on how alcohol prevents heart disease and stroke. It's up to you decide what is right for your life and overall health goal. Two drinks a day is fine if that is your choice. If you currently drink between two and seven drinks a day do not feel pressured to drink less, unless you have a problem with alcohol. Moreover, I am assuming the drinker is following the principles of drinking healthier. Cholesterol studies have shown that low levels of HDL is an independent risk factor for both stroke and heart disease mortality. Therefore, ask your doctor to measure your good cholesterol even if your total cholesterol is less than 200 mg/dl.

As far as eggs are concerned, eat them to your heart's content; they are nature's most perfect food and cheap too! Do not worry about the fat contained in the yolk, but if you're concerned about the fat around your waist, hips, thighs or butt... pay close attention to the next chapter that reveals the truth behind the beer belly!

How to Prevent a Beer Belly and Still Drink Beer!

The whole world is three drinks behind — Humphrey
Bogart

If a beer belly is from too much beer, wine, or liquor, why do
so many non-drinkers have a similar belly? Because drinkers
and non-drinkers both eat similar high-calorie and high-fat
foods, perform similar activities, and consume too many of
their total daily calories just before going to bed. Before I
started drinking healthier my waist was 37 inches and I
weighed 220 pounds. Today, I weigh 155 pounds with a 31-
inch waist and 7 percent body fat. If beer or alcohol caused a
beer belly, I would have developed another one by now! After
all, I have maintained this weight for the last ten years. I drink

more or less the same as before. However, I do not eat the same and that has made all the difference.

I know plenty of drinkers who drink less than I, but have well developed bellies. Moreover, these individuals are branded as heavy drinkers, despite the fact their bellies are from eating too much food. How did I lose my belly and matching love handles and still enjoy the grape, hops, and spirits? By becoming a 21st Century Drinker! And everyone who learns to drink healthier can do the same; it's a simple matter of planning, planning, and more planning. A 21st Century Drinker strategically consumes alcohol and prevents weight gain. Remember the old saying, "You do not own the calories in beer, you only rent them."

Who Said Beer Causes a Beer Belly?

Why was there a need to coin the term "beer belly"? Do we have a specific term for the belly of a non-drinker? No. Even if we believe the non-drinker developed a belly from eating too many Twinkies, we do not call his belly a Twinkie belly. At best we might describe the person as just plain fat. So why do people make reference to beer when they describe a drinker's belly? Is alcohol a scapegoat? Does the falsehood that alcohol makes you fat serve to further another cause, such as the age-old campaign against drinking? Maybe.

When someone uses the term "beer belly" is her intent to describe the drinker's belly? Or is she trying to communicate her contempt for the drinker and the decision to drink? When family members comment on a loved one's belly, do they want the drinker to lose the belly or the desire to drink? If the drinker loses the beer belly, but continues to drink, will that be acceptable?

Clearly, not everyone who uses the term "beer belly" has a hidden agenda. However, the comment still serves to perpetuate the myth that beer is responsible for fat bellies. The beer-belly myth blinds people from seeing the truth. I know plenty of people who choose not to drink out of fear that it causes weight gain. Others mistakenly believe that a drinker with a so-called beer belly spends a considerable amount of time drinking, and must be an alcoholic. This is simply not accurate. When it comes to identifying the culprit behind a huge protuberance, do not point a finger at beer. I once heard a non-drinker state the reason he doesn't drink is because he's afraid of getting a belly like his dad's. Never mind that his dad always washed down each beer with two salami and mayonnaise sandwiches.

Case Study

Ted was a 30-year-old banker and sported a belly that was becoming uncomfortable. Ted never gave any thought to how he drank. Like many people, Ted had no idea how many "base level" calories per day his body required. Nor did he know how many calories he consumed each day. Ted was on the verge of quitting drinking in the mistaken belief that this action would reduce his belly. Luckily, Ted came to see me.

If Ted's goal had been to quit drinking because it was destroying relationships I would have supported that decision. However, his goal was to simply lose his belly, therefore, I suggested that he continue his four to six beer a day regime and apply the principle of "base level" calories. Ted was absolutely stunned, he asked me why this information was not provided by his doctor or HMO. I told him about the reluctance of the medical community, and society as a whole, to come to grips with the fact that a drinker can drink healthier. Nonetheless, eight months later, Ted reported his waist had shrunk from 38 inches to 34. Ted simply followed the information in this book and continued to enjoy his beer each day. Ted also felt that the life-force nutrients allowed him to recuperate faster from a night of drinking.

Beer and alcohol may be rightfully blamed for staining your coffee table or making your breath smell, but your eating habits are to blame if you have a large belly. The next time someone tells you to lose the beer belly, tell him you can't because you're addicted to food! If he thinks you're joking, tell him to buy a copy of this book and let him educate himself.

How to Calculate Your Base-Level Calorie Needs

A drinker must learn to calculate his or her base-level calorie needs. Base level calories are used to perform all of your involuntary activities. The following is a list of involuntary activities your body performs for you each day:

- Heartbeat
- Breathing
- Kidney function
- Blood cell production
- Cellular activities
- Brain functioning.

Each day your body burns an exact number of base-level calories. Your body burns these calories without you ever lifting a finger. This means the base-level calories you eat can never be turned into fat. Calories only form fat when they are "extra." You can never have extra base-level calories because your body always burns all of them up. The number of base-level calories required by your body is based on your age, height, weight, state of health, and percentage of body fat. Ask your physician or local health club to test your body fat using bioelectrical impedance. This test will tell you how many pounds of fat and muscle you carry. It will also reveal your base-level calorie needs. The test takes three minutes at a minimal cost. If you are unable to have this test done, you can determine your base level calorie needs with the Harris-Benedict formula below. This formula is used in hospitals to estimate base level calorie needs:

For Men: 655 + (13.7 x your weight in kilograms) + (5 x your height in centimeters) minus (6.8 x your age)

For Women: 655 + (9.6 x your weight in kilograms) + (1.7 x your height in centimeters) minus (4.7 x your age)

To convert your weight in pounds to kilograms *divide your weight* by 2.2

To convert your height in inches to centimeters, *multiply your height in inches* by 2.54

Every 12 inches = 1 foot. For example, 5 feet = 60 inches (5 feet x 12 inches = 60 inches)
Example: I am 5'10" and weigh 155 pounds.

Step one:
I must convert my weight of 155 pounds into kilograms.
155 pounds divided by 2.2 = 70 kilograms

Step two:
I must convert my height of 70 inches into centimeters.
5'10" is equal to 70 inches. 70 inches multiplied by 2.54 = 178 centimeters

Step three:
I must now plug these numbers into the equation for men.
66 + (13.7 x 70 kilograms = **959**) + (5 x 178 centimeters = **890**) - (6.8 x 36 age = **245**) Total = 66 + 959 + 890 - 245 = **1,670** base level calories per day

Because there are twenty-four hours in a day and sixty minutes in each hour, the total number of minutes in a day equals 1,440 minutes. Therefore, my body burns **1.16 base-level calories per minute.** I calculated this by dividing my base level calories by the number of minutes in a day. For example: 1,670 divided by 1,440 equals **1.16 base-level calories per minute.** Now figure your base level calorie needs. Insert your weight in kilograms, height in centimeters, and age into the formula in the same fashion as in the example above.

Question: Do you mean your body burns 1,670 calories each day even if you stay in bed the entire day?

Answer: Yes, every minute of the day my involuntary activities burn base level calories at a rate of 1.16 calories per minute or 1,670 base level calories each day. The brain alone consumes 400 to 600 base level calories each day. Resting muscles burn a significant amount of base level calories too. As you develop muscle tissue your base level calorie needs increase.

Prove it to yourself. Have your body fat tested using electrical impedance, then work out faithfully over the next two months. Have your body fat tested again. If you developed muscle tissue and lost fat your base level calorie needs will be higher, even if your weight is unchanged. The preferred fuel source of muscles at rest is fat. Therefore, if you increase your muscle mass through exercise, you will increase the amount of fat your body burns each day. Adding muscle to your body allows you to eat and drink more total calories. I cannot stress enough the importance of maintaining or increasing your muscle mass as you age.

Question: What happens if I eat my exact amount of base level calories and perform my daily routine of going to work, shopping, household chores, and exercise?

Answer: You will lose weight. Any voluntary body movements or physical activity of any kind requires additional calories to be consumed, otherwise weight loss occurs.

Question: I want to lose weight. How many calories should I add to my base level calories to cover my physical activity? Do you recommend eating food calories or drinking alcohol calories?

Answer: If you are trying to lose a belly or weight in general you should get all of your base level calories from food. Do not eat any additional food calories above your base level calories. However, you can drink alcohol and not worry about those calories turning to fat.

Question: How come I do not have to worry about the calories in alcohol?

Answer: Remember, all of your base-level calories are burned up performing your involuntary activities. To perform voluntary activities such as walking, general chores, and exercise, your muscles will borrow calories from the involuntary activity budget called base level calories. This creates a base-level calorie deficit which forces your involuntary organs to start burning stored sugar and body fat until the loan is repaid. The loan is repaid when you eat again. Until then, the organs that perform your involuntary activities — heartbeat, breathing, kidney filtering, bone marrow activity, cellular repair and maintenance — will continue to burn stored sugar and fat calories at a set rate per minute.

By performing activities, and not exceeding your base-level calories, your body goes into negative calorie balance. Negative calorie balance means your body fat stores are lower than they were the day before. This is what you want! However, if you consume more than your base-level calories, those extra food calories return you to "normal" or "positive" calorie balance. You do not want this to happen! It means you are just as fat as you were yesterday, or possibly fatter! However, you can drink alcohol instead of eating additional food and still lose fat. Moreover, this option is better than going to bed hungry only to be aroused later by your stomach's cry for food, which prompts you to seek comfort in a bologna sandwich. Clearly, alcohol can be a dieter's best friend.

Question: How can that be? What about all the calories in the alcohol? Wouldn't they cause me to gain weight?

Answer: No. Some of the incoming alcohol calories will be used to meet the minute-by-minute base-level calorie demands of your involuntary organs. Remember, your heart is beating every second of the day and it needs a constant supply of calories. The same goes for the other involuntary organs. Alcohol reduces the amount of stored fat being burned to meet involuntary needs, but it will not stop it like food would. Moreover, alcohol allows you to remain in negative calorie balance.

To make this whole process work like a clock be sure to evenly divide your base-level calories into three or four meals. Choose foods from the best foods listed in Chapter 6 for fastest results, although you will continue to lose weight no matter what you choose as long as you do not exceed your base level calorie needs. If your base-level calorie needs are 1,500, and you want to spend all 1,500 calories on ice cream, you can. However, you cannot have any more food for the rest of the day. They're your calories, and you can spend them any way you want. However, a total junk food diet is not going to provide adequate protein needed to keep you healthy.

Therefore, I suggest you divide your base level calories by four. This will be the amount of calories for each of your four small meals. Next, space the four meals evenly throughout the day. After you have consumed your 1,500 base level calories you can enjoy the free alcohol calories, which have no chance of being stored as fat. This is why 21st Century Drinkers develop a leaner, healthier appearance over time. Refer to the bibliography for research articles that support the fact that alcohol calories do not cause fat gain.

Question: Why is alcohol a poor builder of body fat?

Answer: Before the body can store alcohol as fat, it must first convert alcohol into a non-toxic product. Then it must convert the non-toxic product into a fat molecule. Both of these steps require your body to spend additional calories that were not budgeted. Biochemists use the term *increased metabolic rate* to describe this increased spending of calories. The increase in metabolic rate also creates a base-calorie deficit. Why? Because the calorie cost of the two step alcohol processing is not budgeted into the formulas used to calculate your base-level calorie needs.

Budgeted or not, the liver still must pay those calories as it performs the two step process. Remember muscles are also borrowing base-level calories to perform activities that were not budgeted. Basically, the liver and muscles are stealing base level calories from the involuntary organs. This causes the involuntary organs to steal from body fat and liver sugar. This creates the negative calorie balance as described previously.

Another point of interest is calories from alcohol are not efficiently captured by ATP, a chemical responsible for collecting calories. When alcohol calories are "missed" by ATP, they are released from the body as heat, and never have a chance to be stored as fat. Alcohol disrupts ATP's ability to capture all of its calories and most, especially at higher intakes, escape from the body as heat. Have you ever noticed that drinking makes you feel warm all over? Your cheeks flush as you radiate warmth from your skin. That warmth indicates that ATP is not capturing alcohol calories. Unless the calories are captured by ATP they do not count.

Whereas alcohol is a poor builder of fat, carbohydrate and fat calories are good builders of fat because neither one requires neutralizing. Moreover, carbohydrate is easier or less costly to convert into fat, and fat calories do not require any conversion costs since they are already in the fat molecule form.

Question: I guess what you are saying is calories from alcohol are not equal to calories from carbohydrates or fats?

Answer: Exactly. Calories from fat and carbohydrates are quickly recognized and captured by ATP. After ATP collects a "food" calorie it is labeled for fat storage, or sent to a cell to be burned as energy. If the body has too much food (calories above base level calorie needs), it has too much energy and the extra food calories are readily converted into body fat, whereas alcohol calories are more readily converted into body heat than body fat.

Question: I am trying to lose weight. What if I eat my base-level calorie needs and decide I want to eat extra food calories instead of drinking my alcohol calories?

Answer: You will gain fat. For example, your base-level calorie needs are 1,500 calories per day, and you plan on drinking seven Miller Lites tonight. Each beer contains ninety-six calories, and multiplied by seven, equals a total of 672 additional calories. Your total calorie intake for the day is 1,500 food calories plus 672 alcohol calories = 2,172 total calories.

However, if at the last moment you decide to eat a 672-calorie bacon double cheeseburger instead of the seven beers, will you gain fat? You bet! The fat and carbohydrate calories in the burger will pull you out of negative calorie balance so fast it will make your head spin. If you did this every night you would get fatter. The fat and carbohydrate calories in the burger build body fat more efficiently than the equivalent amount of calories from alcohol. Fat and carbohydrate calories do not know how to escape from the body as heat when the body is obese. Individuals who have less than 8 percent body fat will waste energy during the metabolism of great quantities of food. The muscle appears to dispose of the extra calories before the fat cell has a chance to store them. At least one day a week they can overeat with little consequence in terms of fat gain. I call this the muscle paradox.

Question: It's late at night and I already consumed my base level calorie needs, but I still want something to eat or drink. I am making progress in terms of losing fat and I want to choose the calories that will do the least amount of damage.

What should I eat: 300 calories worth of pie, 300 calories worth of ice cream, or 300 calories worth of alcohol?

Answer: To minimize weight gain and discouragement that will come if you eat food calories, your best choice is to choose 300 calories worth of alcohol. Surprised? How many times have you been told that alcohol was fattening and should be eliminated from a weight loss diet? How many times have you heard, "If you want to lose that belly, stop drinking"? Now you know the truth; alcohol is a poor builder of fat. Nobody can refute this fact. Alcohol is the least fattening source of calories beside pure protein calories such as egg whites, water packed tuna, broiled fish, and skinless turkey or chicken breast.

Reasons Why Alcohol is a Poor Builder of Fat

- Alcohol increases your metabolic rate similar to exercise
- There is a calorie "cost" to "neutralize" alcohol
- There is a calorie "cost" to "convert" alcohol into a fat molecule
- While "converting" alcohol calories into cell energy, ATP fails to capture all the calories, and most escape from the body in the form of heat energy
- As alcohol consumption increases, ATP's ability to capture alcohol calories decreases

Question: What happens to the alcohol calories that are captured by ATP? Will they be labeled for fat storage?

Answer: Anyone who does not exceed his base-level calories will never get fat from drinking additional alcohol calories. Alcohol calories captured by ATP are probably converted to free fatty acids and burned by resting muscle tissue. It would be rare if the body labeled any alcohol calories for fat storage if the base level calories were not exceeded.

Remember, the body must burn calories to convert alcohol into a non-toxic product. After this is accomplished an additional calorie investment is required to convert this non-toxic product into body fat. It's similar to investing in stocks. An investor must pay a commission in order to exchange cash for stock certificates or vice versa. Therefore, right from the start the investment is in the red. Whereas the investor will hopefully move into the black over time, the body can never recoup the alcohol calories lost as heat. The initial calorie "commission" for converting alcohol to a non-toxic product is difficult to determine due to the number of confounding variables.

Question: Would you recommend consuming only 75 percent of base level calories in order to accelerate fat loss?

Answer: Most people need to eat 100 percent of their base level calories from food. Otherwise, they will lack energy, vitality, and health. However, it would be an equally attractive diet choice when compared with the many fast weight loss gimmicks on the market. Many people are so accustomed to eating more than their base level calories that they find it difficult to eat less. I do know some drinkers, myself included, who have lost an appreciable amount of weight by consuming only 75 percent of their base level calorie needs. For example, their base level calorie needs may have been 1,400, but they consumed only 1,050 food calories each day. They lost weight despite drinking an additional 1,000 calories worth of alcohol each day. Only advanced 21st Century Drinkers with a careful eye on their protein and carbohydrate needs can successfully consume less than 100 percent of their base level calories.

Question: Are drinkers who have a large belly eating too many food calories above their base calorie needs, or are they eating too much late at night?

Answer: Yes to both. Nobody sporting a prized belly developed it by drinking beer or any other form of liquor. Many drinkers and non-drinkers alike skip breakfast and lunch and consume their base level calories between 5:00 p.m. and midnight. This style of eating will make you fatter with each passing day. One of the top ten biggest myths is, "If you would stop drinking so much beer you wouldn't have that beer belly." Frequently, this is a desperate attempt from a loved one to persuade a drinker to drink less in hopes that the drinker will decide that giving up beer for a set of washboard abdominals is a healthy trade. Occasionally, and only for a short period of time, the drinker buys this suggestion hook, line, and sinker. However, he realizes time is the only thing being lost and he starts drinking again.

It's unfortunate because the drinker truly believed that giving up drinking would restore his abdominals to a youthful splendor, or at least to a healthier size. The real culprit that goes unchanged is the eating habits. This is precisely why I devoted Chapter 6 along with this chapter to detail the path that leads to a healthier and leaner body. For too many people, food serves as a replacement for love, affection, and friendship. Physiologically, there is no need for you to eat more than 500 calories above your base level calorie amount, unless you are a marathon runner or perform extreme levels of physical activity. If you eat too much I recommend that you identify the source of unhappiness in your life. If you can solve this problem you will be able to drop your fat with little effort.

Question: What are the real culprits behind the so-called beer belly?

Answer: Lack of knowledge. Most drinkers have no idea how many base level calories they need. They often lack an organized exercise program. Sorry, mowing the lawn and doing house or yard work is not organized exercise. It is tiring work, but it does not increase muscle mass nor stamina, both of which many drinkers lack. Remember, only muscle tissue burns fat while you are sleeping. Therefore, if you exercise, your body will become more efficient at burning fat. I truly believe that my devotion to working out is part of my successful ability to drink healthier.

Question: How come most skid row alcoholics are very thin even though they drink thousands of alcohol calories each day?

Answer: Drinkers who drink thousands of calories each day are usually malnourished. They simply do not eat the amount of food calories required to gain weight, and they lack sufficient life-force nutrients. Heavy drinking fully disables ATP's from capturing alcohol calories and not one ounce of weight gain occurs. I know drinkers who drink 3,000 calories a day and are thin or at low normal weight.

Clearly, if this was 3,000 food calories they would be heavier. However, the drinker does not gain weight since the calories are from alcohol. Occasionally, and especially during the holidays, I consume 1,000 or more calories from alcohol and never gain a pound. For me it's just a change of pace and time to let loose. No harm comes to me or anyone else because it is strategically planned drinking with no margin for being an amateur.

The Real Culprits Behind the Fat Belly

- Failure to know and follow your base calorie needs
- Eating fat or carbohydrate calories in excess of your base calorie needs
- Eating the "worst" foods after a night of drinking
- Eating one or two big meals per day, instead of eating four or five smaller meals
- Lack of consistent (three times a week) workouts with weights
- Lack of abdominal muscle training and aerobic activity
- Peanuts and all other nuts
- Potato chips
- Corn chips
- Creamy dips
- Chicken wings
- Other fried meat or snack food
- Pizza
- Fatty meat sandwiches: salami, pepperoni, sausage, pastrami, corned beef, bologna
- Cheese
- Salad dressing and mayonnaise

Exercise Techniques That Improve Your Waistline

Of course before starting any exercise program you should first consult your doctor and share your goal for working out. After receiving your doctor's approval think about joining a gym or purchasing some home weight lifting equipment.

- *Hanging leg raises:* Simply hang from an overhead bar and bring your knees up to your chest. At first you may only be able to do one or two. Stick with it and after a week you should be doing ten with no sweat. Perform this exercise three times daily for as many repetitions as possible.

- *Side bends:* Stand with feet shoulder-width apart, hands to your sides, and bend to your left, back to starting position, and bend to your right. Perform this exercise twice daily, performing fifty repetitions on each side.

- *Crunches:* Lie on the floor, feet flat, and knees bent with your hands behind your head. Keeping your lower back flat on the floor, curl your upper body until your shoulder blades almost leave the floor. Perform this exercise three times daily for as many repetitions as possible.

- *Jogging:* Jog or walk one mile twice a week.

- *Ab-roller:* For a good workout buy an Ab-roller and follow the directions. An Ab-roller is a popular and inexpensive piece of exercise equipment that isolates the abdominal muscles.

A Final Word of Encouragement

If you never exercise, this will be an initial hardship for you. However, it is an investment in yourself. The 21st Century Drinkers who are in good shape enjoy their drinking more than out-of-shape drinkers. Trust me, this is true. More importantly, drinkers who have additional muscle mass can tolerate alcohol better than fat drinkers. Why? Because well muscled drinkers have a greater amount of total body water. This means they are less likely to become dehydrated, and the additional body water helps dilute the alcohol in their system. It's just like adding water to a shot of alcohol; the water will dilute the strength of the alcohol making it taste weaker.

When alcohol enters the body of a muscular person, the additional body water dilutes the alcohol's effect on the drinker. The idea that a heavier body weight allows you to drink more is a fallacy, the *extra muscle mass* and not fat is responsible for this phenomena. I know plenty of people who weigh considerably more than I do, however, and I am not proud, but I can drink them under the table. Why? Because I have more pounds of muscle than they do. Overall, they are heavier in weight, but their weight is mostly fat, and mine is mostly muscle. Remember, fat tissue is virtually water-free and muscle tissue is mostly water.

I sincerely encourage each drinker to take action today and start implementing the information learned thus far. Take a moment now and calculate your base level calorie needs and get started down the road to drinking healthier!

Chapter 9
Helping the One You Love to Become
a 21st Century Drinker
157

Helping the One You Love to Become a 21st Century Drinker

Habit is habit, and not to be flung out the window by any man, but coaxed downstairs a step at a time. — Mark Twain

When it comes to the health of your loved one, your advice can be simply stated: *caveat emptor* or let the drinker beware. But, be careful! The goal is to get your loved one to drink healthier, not to make him or her run in the other direction. Once a person realizes she is being asked simply to drink healthier, she is all ears. Some heavy drinkers and alcoholics accustomed to being told to quit drinking find it shocking that they are not being asked to quit. At first glance they may or may not want to make the effort to drink healthier. Others who drink only moderately or occasionally may feel they do not need to take life-force nutrients. You know they do!

Many drinkers will think it's a message sent down from heaven and race out to the store with their list in hand. To a greater or lesser extent all drinkers will entertain the thought of drinking healthier, because most people do not want to hurt themselves if they can help it. Moreover, drinking healthier allows the drinker to continue enjoying an old national pastime with less injury. No drinker wants to wake up in the morning knowing his health is slowly going down the tubes. The important point to remember is that no matter how much or how little your loved one drinks, he or she will benefit from the appropriate level of life-force nutrients.

If Your Loved One is an Alcoholic

Alcoholics often keep any health problems to themselves out of fear they will be reminded that it's their own fault. This is unfortunate because nobody should have to suffer with health problems that are a result of insufficient life-force nutrients.

If you mention that you want him to take vitamins, the drinker is apt to say he does not need them. Or he may tell you he feels fine. This is all part of the self-defense that developed from years of having to say he feels fine when he does not. How many times has a drinker heard, "I hope you feel sick in the morning"? Better yet, how often has he heard, "You wouldn't feel so bad if you didn't drink so much"? There are a hundred variations, but they all send the same message which is, "It's your own fault that you feel sick or have an alcohol-related health problem." True, it is the drinker's fault. However, mentioning this only makes him deny that he feels sick. For example, if a drinker knows that a loved one will make one of the above comments, he prepares an answer ahead of time which is, "I feel fine, I'm not sick, just a little tired." Therefore, you must approach your loved one like a salesperson. Sell him something he really needs; make it his decision to buy. Then he will be more likely to follow the steps towards drinking healthier. If he feels it's your decision, it will probably be a no go.

Comments That Discourage Your Loved One From Drinking Healthier

- You should take these "pills" until you decide to quit drinking

- You drink too much, so you should take these "pills"

- Taking these "pills" might be a new beginning or step towards recovery

- Drinking is bad for your health, so you need to take these "pills"

- Promise me you will not forget to take these "pills"

- Take these "pills" or you will end up like... *Do not call life-force nutrients "pills," it sounds too much like a medication. I use the term for convenience when writing rather than naming each nutrient capsule. However, I do not use it when I am working with clients.*

Comments That Encourage Your Loved One to Drink Healthier

- I was wrong, drinking does not make a person fat
- Research shows drinkers can stay healthier if they take special nutrients
- Drinkers who take life-force nutrients are less likely to develop liver damage
- Drinkers who take life-force nutrients are less likely to get hangovers
- Too bad Uncle Sandy is not alive, he would have benefited from this book
- I can increase my good cholesterol by drinking wine, beer, or spirits
- Have you heard about the new book *Drink as Much as You Want and Live Longer?*
- I am going to start taking life-force nutrients to protect my liver from toxic enemies
- I just read that certain foods when consumed with alcohol cause a hangover
- Do you want to try an experiment?
- I think you should become a 21st Century Drinker

Any of the above can successfully engage you into conversation with your loved one. They are all non-threatening and definitely thought provoking. I have tested these phrases and found them to be excellent ice-breakers with even the most headstrong drinker.

Chapter 9
Helping the One You Love to Become
a 21st Century Drinker
161

A Gentle Approach

After your initial approach using one of the above opening lines, do not mention how much your loved one drinks. Every drinker is well aware of how much he drinks. Tell him something he does not know. Begin with the concept of drinking healthier. Do not be surprised if he thinks you are trying to fool him with "pills" that will dull their "taste" for alcohol. Too many treatments are based on that very principle. Reassure the drinker that this is not a trick and your intent is to make her drinking more pleasurable. For an authoritative impact show her this book, let her read it, or read it to her. Allow her to see that you are not asking her to quit. You must sincerely approach your loved one with only one intent in mind. And that intent is to help him or her to drink healthier.

You will never be able to influence the drinker to quit. That is a well known cold hard fact. Quitting is something only he or she can decide. Therefore, settle for the next best thing, and that is a healthier loved one. You can add years to your loved one's life, and more importantly to improving the quality of life. Therefore, the time is now to convince your loved one to drink healthier. After reading this chapter it should be an easy sell, because the concept sells itself. It does not make sense to drink any other way. Your loved one will have no excuse not to drink healthier.

Selling the Concept of Drinking Healthier

Drinking places demands on the body like a race driver places demands on a race car. The difference is the race car was built and maintained to handle that excessive wear and tear. If you asked your loved one if it made sense to use high performance racing oil in a race car, the odds are he would answer "yes."

He realizes a race car performs at higher than normal speeds, and the engine can reach extreme temperatures. Ordinary oil and fuel would cause the race car to under perform when put to the test on race day. As sure as unleaded gas and 10w40 motor oil is insufficient for a race car engine, regular food will cause the drinker to under perform physically and mentally.

No race car driver, or any driver for that matter, would run an engine without protective oil to lubricate the moving metal parts. The body of a drinker is more valuable than any car on earth, and drinking without life-force nutrient protection is exactly like running an engine without oil in it. There can be only one outcome, internal damage. Alcohol damages an unprotected body in a similar fashion as racing damages an unprotected engine.

Examples like this help your loved one to take the first step towards drinking healthier. By viewing her body as high-performance equipment, a drinker recognizes the need to ingest *special protective substances.* It works because every drinker truly wants to be ready on race day. Which for many drinkers is each and every day!

Ask your loved one how he would fight a fire if he was an experienced professional firefighter. Would that person approach the fire without fire gear on? Of course not. The defense would be to protect the skin with special gear which includes a respirator, fire coat, gloves, boots, and helmet. The offense would be a fire hose and a proven strategy to put out the fire without injury. Drinkers do not realize that drinking without life-force nutrient protection is like being caught in an inferno without the protective gear and skill of a firefighter. This should be a convincing analogy, because you already

Chapter 9
Helping the One You Love to Become
a 21st Century Drinker
163

know each sip of beer, wine, and liquor is like a small fire that must be snuffed out by the liver. The firefighter's offense against a fire is the fire hose. The drinker's defense and offense against alcohol is the correct level of life-force nutrients. Fire fighting and unprotected drinking are both dangerous activities. However, the professional firefighter is the only one receiving financial compensation for his or her risk. Your loved one knowingly accepts all the risks and receives no reward. Nothing! The next step is to get your loved one to actually act on this startling new discovery.

Getting Started: Taking Supplements Together — the Buddy System

The amount your loved one drinks will determine which level of life-force nutrients are needed. Your goal should be to enable your loved one to follow the level of life-force nutrient protection that corresponds with his level of consumption. However, any level of life-force nutrient protection is better than none. Therefore, a sub-level could be a starting point for drinkers who are less than enthusiastic about taking supplements.

Implementing a new change is difficult even if it provides benefits. This is why your loved one needs your support. Start by buying life-force nutrients for yourself and start taking them in your loved one's presence. Showing a personal interest in drinking healthier will have a positive impact. Your interest sends a clear message that you accept the drinking and only desire to keep your loved one healthy. Your new passion is bound to be noticed. Demonstrate your ability to drink healthier by taking a life-force nutrient while enjoying a glass of wine, or other alcohol beverage. Eventually, your loved one will pop the question, "Why are you taking those vitamins?" Boom. You're there and in short order you can sell the concept hook, line, and sinker.

Another strategy is to enlist the help and support of one or two of your loved one's drinking associates. Too often we are influenced rightly or wrongly by the actions and behaviors of those we look up to or share a certain bond with. Your loved one probably has a friend who would be most enthusiastic about the idea of drinking healthier. Remember, take advantage of the rebel-like nature of drinking healthier. Before this book no one believed or even considered the fact that a drinker could drink healthier. Therefore, the quote by Walter Bagehot used in the introduction bears repeating, "The great pleasure in life is doing what other people say you cannot do." This is very powerful in terms of getting your loved one and possibly one or two of his friends to drink healthier. People can be driven to succeed by the voices that say they cannot. In this case the voices are coming from the anti-drinking establishment.

Believe me when I say if you can get an influential drinker to start drinking healthier, she can sell it to the world. I know drinkers who mimic the lifestyle of their drinking friends. It's really no different than people being persuaded to eat or drink the choice of champions, or wear athletic shoes that are endorsed by popular athletes. Modeling behavior is an easy way to get your loved one to drink healthier. Think hard and long and you will find the right model to help your loved one to drink healthier.

Chapter 9
Helping the One You Love to Become
a 21st Century Drinker
165

On Their Own: Sending Your Son
or Daughter Off to College

It's a fact your son or daughter will be drinking. Wouldn't you sleep better knowing your child, away from home for the first time, is able to drink healthier? Believe me when I say the majority of college students drink. Actually, drink is not an accurate term when it comes to college age drinkers; guzzle is probably closer to the mark. I remember how much I drank in college and it still frightens me. I would have listened with great interest if my parents sat me down and tutored me in the finer points of becoming a 21st Century Drinker.

Drinkers of all ages and backgrounds do not have a clue as to how many nutrients are destroyed by alcohol. *Drink as Much as You Want and Live Longer* should be required reading for all drinkers, young and old. The likelihood of your son or daughter being involved in a drinking contest is highest between the ages of 16 and 21.

I am totally against trying to establish or break drinking records. Moreover, nobody should allow himself to be a part of a drinking competition. Any drinker can drink himself to death. The real measure of a drinker is the ability to live a long productive life, while in constant company of the grape, hops, and spirits without being weakened. Drinking is not a game, it is a serious activity with serious consequences if abused. Your son or daughter needs to be informed of the damage which alcohol can cause in the hands of an amateur drinker.

You have protected your children many times when they were growing up. You gave good advice such as brush your teeth to prevent cavities, don't play in a busy street, wear reflective clothing when bicycling at night, wear a helmet, don't talk or go with a stranger, and other pearls of wisdom.

You gave all this advice and more to reduce their chances of being harmed. You have the power in your hands to prevent children from ever experiencing the ravages of unprotected drinking. Teach them right from the start how to drink healthier.

Case Study

Harry knew his wife Connie drank way too much, but she was unwilling to seek help and certainly was not going to be coaxed into abstinence. Harry attended a corporate wellness program I gave and asked if I could help his wife to drink healthier. I told him I would help her stay healthy until she was ready to seek help or learned to hold a job. Connie's problem was not that she drank, but that she allowed her drinking to affect her ability to work the next day. In the last year she had lost three jobs due to lateness and absenteeism. At first, Connie thought the whole thing was some kind of joke or that I was going to force her to drink alcohol until she got sick. After thirty minutes of explaining my intentions, Connie began to relax and ponder my proposal. When she realized my goal was to protect her health despite her continued drinking she burst into tears. It was a very emotional moment for everyone. Here was a woman who had been neglected by the health profession for years, and now was going to be ministered nutritionally for the first time!

With little coaxing, Connie purchased the necessary life-force nutrients and started to shield her body from alcohol's harm. She stashed life-force nutrients in her car's glove compartment, her purse, at her mom's house, everywhere and anywhere she had them readily available. Connie followed each step as best she could and Harry encouraged her each step of the way. My program eliminated the stress that previously consumed their relationship, and they grew closer and learned how to nurture each other in a new way. The whole process was a total healing experience. After six months Connie found a new job and has been a productive employee for more than two years. Her feelings of fatigue and the awful hangovers are in the past. In fact, she now cashes in her unused sick time each year, and Harry and Connie treat themselves to a romantic vacation.

Chapter 9
Helping the One You Love to Become
a 21st Century Drinker
167

I wonder if we asked an older drinker, besieged with alcohol-related health problems, if she wished she could have learned to drink healthier during her youth. I bet she would certainly say "yes." If given the opportunity to go back to my youth, to take better care of my teeth, I would go. Maybe then I would not be enduring the pain and expense of my fourth crown!

One of the best gifts besides love that you can give to your children is the power of knowledge. You must trust their judgment. Now it's time to break out the blender and learn the best drinks life has to offer.

Drink Recipes:
How to Make 21st Century Drinks

No pleasure lasts long unless there is variety in it. —
Publilius Syrus

Nothing soothes an overworked brain cell better than a little
nectar of the gods. With so many new drinks being concocted
daily it is hard to keep up with the latest in mixology. For the
most part ordering a "trendy" drink in a bar or restaurant is a
$5 gamble. Therefore, I suggest you learn to make your own
21st Century Drinks at home. Then you will know exactly how
your drink should taste.

Entertaining at Home

First you need to stock your bar, may I suggest the basics?

Spirits	Mixers
Tequila	Clearly Canadian flavored water
Rum	Diet Coke and Diet Sprite
Vodka	Dole Pineapple-Orange
Scotch	Club soda and water
Gin	
Whiskey or Bourbon	

Wine
Chardonnay
Zinfandel
Merlot

Liqueurs for Half-Shots

½ Malibu Rum and ½ rum
½ Tia Maria and ½ tequila
½ Kahlua and ½ vodka
½ Frangelico and ½ tequila or vodka

Ice
Always have plenty of ice on hand. I see too many drinks being made without enough ice. Ice is the first thing you put into the glass when you make any drink.

Garnishes
Buy a large jar of Maraschino cherries and drain half the juice out and replace it with vodka. Let the jar sit in your

refrigerator for two weeks. Anytime you have a sore throat or desire to sweeten a drink take one tablespoon.

Lemon	Pineapple
Lime	Maraschino cherries
Orange	Olives

Slice the fruit into ⅛-inch slices and then cut them in half. You can place the garnish on the rim or inside the drink.

Accessories
  Blender
  Juicer
  Stainless steel mixing cup
  Drink stirrers
  Bar napkins

Clearly, you do not need all of the above. They are only suggestions if you entertain often and your guests have broad drinking interests.

Improving a Cheap Bottle of Wine

Let's face it, the gift bottle of wine you received last year for Christmas may not be drinking quality. However, that does not mean you have to throw it out, or re-circulate it as a gift to someone else. You can turn that underdeveloped grape extract into the nectar of the gods by making spritzers, which is a fancy name for mixing wine with a non-alcohol beverage.

How to do it:

Mix the wine (red or white) with an equal portion of diet Sprite or Clearly Canadian flavored water. The flavors of Clearly Canadian that marry the wine best are:

Strawberry-Melon	Green Apple
Raspberry Cream	Wild Cherry
Mountain Blackberry	Tangerine

Wine Advice: You Cannot go Wrong With These!

Vouvray: Domaine de Vaufuget 1996
Rosé: Barton & Guestier Rosé d'Anjou 1996
Chenin Blanc: Champalou Cuvee des Fondraux
La Nobleraie Muscadet: Sevre et Maine Sur Lie 1997
White Zinfandel: Deloach Vineyards 1997
Pinot Gris: King Estate Winery 1996
Sauvignon Blanc: Chatueau Ste. Michelle 1996, Washington
 State
Cabernet Sauvignon: Silver Oaks Cellars, 1993

If these wines are tough to pronounce, bring this book to your local wine merchant and allow her to assist you.

Give Diet Soda a Try!

Diet soda can be mixed with any of your favorite spirits. Again, if you do not like "diet" learn to acquire a taste for it. Most people can accomplish this within three weeks. Give it a try! Remember, if you're trying to lose weight you should not be using sugar-containing beverages as your mixer. This means you need to stick with club soda, water, and diet soda if you need a mixer.

Marriages Made in Heaven:
Flavored Waters and Spirits

Flavored water imparts a better flavor to a drink than club soda or water and even contains less calories than regular soda. That is why I recommend Clearly Canadian flavored water. Of course you can choose any brand of flavored carbonated water and still make a good drink taste better.

FRENCH MARTINI
Fill a 10 oz. glass with ice
1.5 oz. vodka
3 oz. Cherry Clearly Canadian
Strain into a glass.

COOL BREEZE
Fill a 10 oz. glass with ice
1.5 oz. rum
½ oz. Malibu rum
3 oz. Strawberry-Melon Clearly Canadian
Add two maraschino cherries.

IRISH WHISKEY FLOAT
Add 5-6 ice cubes to an empty blender
1.5 oz. Irish whiskey or Scotch whiskey
2 oz. of ginger ale
2 oz. Mountain Blackberry Clearly Canadian
½ scoop of lime sherbet
Blend until smooth.

21ST CENTURY MARGARITA
10 oz. ice-filled glass
1.5 oz. tequila
1½ oz. sweet-n-sour mix
½ oz. Grand Marnier or Triple Sec
Hand shake and strain into a glass
Add a lime twist.

21ST CENTURY VEGAS TEA
10 oz. ice-filled glass
½ oz. Maraschino cherry vodka
½ oz. vodka
½ oz. rum
½ oz. Malibu Rum
½ oz. tequila
4 oz. sweet-n-sour mix
3 oz. diet Coke
Add a lemon twist and a maraschino cherry.

Give a New Meaning to the Term JUICER

A juicer is a worthwhile investment that allows you to make creative concoctions that have real health benefits. I will offer a few drink recipes that I make with my juicer. I recommend sticking primarily to fruits. However, you should explore a wide variety of fruit and vegetable combinations because each drinker has a unique palate.

Root vegetables such as beets, (a known liver cleanser), could be mellowed with a fruit or fruit juice to marry well with spirits. Other vegetables alone such as tomatoes, cucumbers, and celery or combined together could be mixed directly with iced spirits.

After you make the recipes below, add one to three table-spoons of the *mixture* to your favorite drink. The vegetable and fruit mixture will add important life-force nutrients to the body. You may not like all the combinations. Therefore, create your own signature blend by juicing those fruits and vegetables you find appealing.

To fortify a drink, start by adding ⅛ of a teaspoon of liquid B-complex. Of all the mixers I tried, Clearly Canadian seems to hide the vitamin taste the best. Fortifying alcohol with vitamins is not a new idea. However, do not expect the government to sign an enrichment act like they did for white bread. Juicing and fortifying allow immediate absorption. The digestive system does not have to separate the nutrients from the food or drink since this function has already been performed.

RASPBERRY DREAM

Juice 1 beet leaf , ¼ beet, ½ slice lime, and 1 plum
Add 2 tablespoons of the mixture to a 10 oz. ice-filled glass.
1.5 oz. vodka and 3 oz. diet Sprite
Hand-shake or stir briskly
Add 1/8 teaspoon of liquid B-complex to the *Raspberry Dream* and you have made a *Bloody Dream*.

ALPINE AVALANCHE
Juice ¼ clove of garlic, 1 lime slice, 1 apple, and ¼ carrot
Add two tablespoons of the mixture into 10 oz. ice-filled
  glass
1.5 oz. rum and 3 oz. diet Coke or diet Sprite
Hand-shake or stir briskly.

GINGER APPLE
Juice 1 apple, $1/8^{th}$ inch fresh ginger root, and 6 pineapple
  cubes
Pour mixture into a 10 oz. ice-filled glass
1.5 oz. rum and 3 oz. diet Coke or diet Sprite.
Hand-shake or stir briskly.

FRUITY PINK LEMONADE
Juice 2 radishes and add to a 10 oz. ice-filled glass
1.5 oz. vodka
1 teaspoon Triple Sec
3 oz. Strawberry-melon Clearly Canadian
Hand-shake or stir briskly.

PUMPKIN SMASH
Juice ½ apple, ⅛ carrot and add to a 10 oz. ice-filled glass
1.5 oz. vodka
3 oz. Strawberry-Melon Clearly Canadian
Add a dash of nutmeg and cinnamon
Hand-shake or stir briskly.

Adding ZING With Cayenne Pepper

COYOTE MARY
Fill a 10 oz. glass with ice
1.5 oz. tequila
3 oz. pineapple-orange juice
1.5 oz. V-8 juice
1/8 teaspoon cayenne pepper
Hand-shake or stir briskly, add a lime twist. Strain if desired.

CHEYENNE SUNRISE
10 oz. ice-filled glass
1.5 oz. tequila
1.5 oz. pineapple-orange juice
1/8 teaspoon cayenne pepper
1 teaspoon Triple-Sec
1 teaspoon Amaretto
½ to 1 teaspoon Grenadine
1 teaspoon sweet and sour mix
Hand-shake or stir briskly.

MARGARITA CAYENNE
10 oz. ice-filled glass
2 oz. margarita mix
1.5 oz. tequila
1 teaspoon extra dry vermouth
1/8 teaspoon cayenne pepper
Hand-shake or stir briskly.

COCONUT CANDY
10 oz. ice-filled glass
1.5 oz. vodka
3 oz. fresh green apple juice
2 tablespoons fresh coconut juice
2 oz. Alpine Berry Clearly Canadian or 2 oz. diet Sprite
Hand-shake or stir briskly. Add a lime twist.

THE MOUNTAINEER
8 oz. ice-filled glass
1.5 oz. Seagrams 7
3 oz. Mountain Blackberry Clearly Canadian
Hand-shake or stir briskly.

THE SLINGER
8 oz. ice-filled glass
1.5 oz. rum
3 oz. Strawberry-Melon Clearly Canadian
Hand-shake or stir briskly. Add a lime twist.

GOLD PESO
8 oz. ice-filled glass
1.5 oz. gold tequila
3 oz. Alpine Fruit & Berry Clearly Canadian
Hand-shake or stir briskly. Add a lime or lemon twist.

TANGO
8 oz. ice-filled glass
1.5 oz. vodka
2 oz. orange juice
2 oz. diet Sprite
1 teaspoon Grenadine
Hand-shake or stir briskly.

OASIS
10 oz. ice-filled glass
1.5 oz. tequila
1 teaspoon Amaretto
2.5 oz. fresh pineapple juice
2 oz. Alpine Fruit & Berry Clearly Canadian
Hand-shake or stir briskly.

DC FINE & DRY
10 oz. ice-filled glass
1.5 oz. vodka
1 oz. very dry vermouth
Hand-shake or stir briskly
Squeezed lime slice.

DC FINE & DRY II
As above plus:
1 tablespoon fresh coconut juice
3 oz. Mountain Berry Clearly Canadian

THE NIHONJIN
8 oz. of sugar-free hot cocoa
1 oz. of peppermint schnapps
A loving sprinkle of cinnamon

Snacks That Mix Well With Alcohol

Baked potato crisps
Pretzels
Chex cereals
Microwave light popcorn

A Final Thought

A Sip for the Angels

It is never a waste
In fact it's a sign of good taste
You never quite know when an angel shall pass
So leave the last swallow in the glass
Set it aside for a moment or two
And an angel just may smile down upon you
Alcohol evaporates into thin air
You cannot see this no matter how hard you stare
But in the eye of an angel, it's a sign you care
by Fred Beyerlein

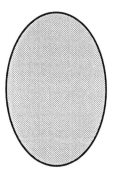

Bibliography

Chapter 1

"Carnitine Metabolism in B12 Deficiency." *Nutrition Reviews*, March 1989: pp. 89-91.

Diamond, Ivan and Robert O. Messing. "Neurologic Effects of Alcoholism." *Western Journal of Medicine*, September 1994: pp. 279-87.

"Dietary Choline and Synaptic Morphology in Mice." *Nutrition Reviews*, January 1987: pp. 25-7.

"Fermentable Fibers and Vitamin B12 Dependency." *Nutrition Reviews*, April 1991: pp. 119-20.

Fleming, Robert. "Medical Treatment of the Inebriate." *Alcohol, Science and Society*. New Haven, Conn. Journal of Studies on Alcohol, Inc., 1945: pp. 387-401.

Gambert, Steven R. "Alcohol Abuse: Medical Effects of Heavy Drinking in Late Life." *Geriatrics*, June 1997: pp. 30-7.

Gloria, Luisa et al. "Nutritional Deficiencies in Chronic Alcoholics: Relation to Dietary Intake and Alcohol Consumption." *The American Journal of Gastroenterology*, March 1997: pp. 485-89.

Kubow, Stan. "Lipid Oxidation Products in Food and Atherogenesis." *Nutrition Reviews*, February 1993: pp. 33-40.

Lambert, D. et al. "Alcoholic Cirrhosis and Cobalamin Metabolism." *Digestion*, 58, 1997: pp. 64-71.

Lieber, Charles S. "Alcohol and the Liver: 1994 Update." *Gastroenterology*, April 1994: pp. 1085-1105.

Lieber, Charles S. "Ethanol Metabolism, Cirrhosis and Alcoholism." *Clinca Chimica Acta*, January 1997: pp. 59-84.

Lieber, Charles S. "The Influence of Alcohol on Nutritional Status." *Nutrition Reviews*, July 1988: pp. 241-54.

Lindenbaum, J. et al. "Neuropsychiatric Disorders Caused by Cobalamin Deficiency in Absence of Anemia or Macrocytosis." *The New England Journal of Medicine*, June 1988: pp. 1720-28.

Mainous, Mark R. et al. "Nutritional Support of the Gut: How and Why?" *New Horizons*, May 1994: pp. 193-201.

"Methyl Group Deficiency: Effects on One-Carbon Unit and Folate Metabolism." *Nutrition Reviews*, December 1989: pp. 375-77.

Meydani, Simin N. "Vitamin/Mineral Supplementation, the Aging Immune Response and Risk of Infection." *Nutrition Reviews*, April 1993: pp. 106-09.

Morencos, F. Casafont et al. "Small Bowel Bacterial Overgrowth in Patients with Alcoholic Cirrhosis." *Digestive Diseases and Sciences*, June 1995: pp. 1252-56.

Nielsen, Forrest H. "Nutritional Significance of the Ultratrace Elements." *Nutrition Reviews*, October 1988: pp. 337-41.

"Nutritional Management of Cirrhosis." *Nutrition Reviews*, July 1988: pp. 259-62.

"Postoperative Hypophosphatemia: A Multifactorial Problem." *Nutrition Reviews*, April 1989: pp. 111-16.

Quigley, Eamonn M. M. "Gastrointestinal Dysfunction in Liver Disease and Portal Hypertension." Editorial. *Digestive Diseases and Sciences*, March 1996: pp. 557-61.

Rall, Laura C. et al. "Vitamin B6 and Immune Incompetence." *Nutrition Reviews*, August 1993: pp. 217-25.

Reynolds, Telfer B. and Gary C. Kanel. "Alcoholic Liver Disease." *Internal Medicine*. 1st ed. Jay H. Stein et al. Boston: Little, Brown and Co., 1983: pp. 203-09.

Tjandra, Bernard S. and Rudi A. Janknegt. "Neurogenic Impotence and Lower Urinary Tract Symptoms Due to Vitamin B1 Deficiency in Chronic Alcoholism." *The Journal of Urology*, March 1997: pp. 954-55.

"Unrecognized Cobalamin-Responsive Neuropsychiatric Disorders." *Nutrition Reviews*, July 1989: pp. 208-10.

Zubaran, C. et al. "Wernicke-Korsakoff Syndrome." *Postgraduate Medical Journal*, January 1997: pp. 27-31.

Chapter 4

Ahmed, Shameem et al. "Interactions Between Alcohol and Beta-Carotene in Patients with Alcoholic Liver Disease." *American Journal of Clinical Nutrition*, September 1994: pp. 430-36.

Caregaro, Lorenza et al. "Malnutrition in Alcoholic and Virus-Related Cirrhosis." *American Journal of Clinical Nutrition*, April 1996: pp. 602-09.

"Nutritional Management of Cirrhosis." *Nutrition Reviews*, July 1988: pp. 259-62.

Clot, P. et al. "Monitoring Oxidative Damage in Patients with Liver Cirrhosis and Different Daily Alcohol Intake." *Gut*, November 1994: pp. 1637-43.

"Inhibition of Free Radical Chain Oxidation by Alpha-Tocopherol and Other Plasma Antioxidants." *Nutrition Reviews*, May 1988: pp. 206-07.

Kinney P. L. et al. "Biomarkers of Lung Inflammation in Recreational Joggers Exposed to Ozone." *American Journal of Respiratory and Critical Care Medicine*, November 1996: pp. 1430-35.

Kubow, Stan. "Lipid Oxidation Products in Food and Athero-genesis." *Nutrition Reviews*, February 1993: pp. 33-40.

Lieber, Charles S. "Alcohol and the Liver: 1994 Update." *Gastroenterology*, April 1994: pp. 1085-1105.

Lieber, Charles S. "The Influence of Alcohol on Nutritional Status." *Nutrition Reviews*, July 1988: pp. 241-54.

Lieber, Charles S. "Ethanol Metabolism, Cirrhosis and Alco-holism." *Clinca Chimica Acta*, January 1997: pp. 59-84.

Mitchell, Mack C. and H. Franklin Herlong. "Alcohol and Nu-trition: Caloric Value, Bioenergetics, and Relationship to Liver Damage." *Annual Review Nutrition*, June 1986: pp. 457-74.

Nielsen, Forrest H. "Nutritional Significance of the Ultratrace Elements." *Nutrition Reviews*, October 1988: pp. 337-41.

"Nutritional Management of Cirrhosis." *Nutrition Reviews*, July 1988: pp. 259-62.

Teli, Mohd R. et al. "Determinants of Progression to Cirrhosis or Fibrosis in Pure Alcoholic Fatty Liver." *The Lancet*, October 1995: pp. 987-90.

Van Gossum, Andre et al. "Deficiency in Antioxidant Factors in Patients with Alcohol-Related Chronic Pancreatitis." *Di-gestive Diseases and Sciences*, June 1996: pp. 1225-31.

Chapter 5

Ahmed, Shameem et al. "Interactions Between Alcohol and Beta-Carotene in Patients with Alcoholic Liver Disease." *American Journal of Clinical Nutrition*, September 1994: pp. 430-36.

Lieber, Charles S. "Alcohol and the Liver: 1994 Update." *Gastroenterology*, April 1994: pp. 1085-1105.

Lieber, Charles S. "Ethanol Metabolism, Cirrhosis and Alcoholism." *Clinca Chimica Acta*, January 1997: pp. 59-84.

Lieber, Charles S. "The Influence of Alcohol on Nutritional Status." *Nutrition Reviews*, July 1988: pp. 241-54.

Chapter 6

Low, A. G. "Nutritional Regulation of Gastric Secretion, Digestion and Emptying." *Nutrition Research Reviews*, March 1990: pp. 229-52.

Morencos, F. Casafont et al. "Small Bowel Bacterial Overgrowth in Patients with Alcoholic Cirrhosis." *Digestive Diseases and Sciences*, June 1995: pp. 1252-56.

Chapter 7

Cravo, Marilia L. et al. "Homocysteinemia in Chronic Alcoholism: Correlation with Folate, Vitamin B-12, and Vitamin B-6 Status." *The American Journal of Clinical Nutrition*, February 1996: pp. 220-24.

"Dietary Choline and Synaptic Morphology in Mice." *Nutrition Reviews*, January 1987: pp. 25-7.

Dillner, Luisa et al. "Alcohol — Pushing the Limits." *British Medical Journal*, January 1996: pp. 7-9.

Gronbaek, Morten and Thorkild I. A. Sorensen. "Alcohol Consumption and Risk of Coronary Heart Disease." *British Medical Journal*, August 1996: p. 365.

Heins, Hans O. et al. "Alcohol Consumption, Serum Low Density Lipoprotein Cholesterol Concentration, and Risk of Ischaemic Heart Disease: Six Year Follow Up in the Copenhagen Male Study." *British Medical Journal*, March 1996: pp. 736-41.

"Inhibition of LDL Oxidation by Phenolic Substances in Red Wine: A Clue to the French Paradox?" *Nutrition Reviews*, June 1993: pp. 185-87.

Kessaris, Nicos et al. "Few People will Change Their Drinking Habits in London..." Letter. *British Medical Journal*, January 1996: p. 2.

Lambert, D. et al. "Alcoholic Cirrhosis and Cobalamin Metabolism." *Digestion*, 58, 1997: pp. 64-71.

Le Fanu, James. "Civil Servants Should Be Congratulated for Rejecting Whole Population Theory." *British Medical Journal*, January 1996: p. 1.

"Magnesium Deficiency and Ischemic Heart Disease." *Nutrition Reviews*, September 1988: pp. 311-12.

McNamara, Donald J. "Dietary Cholesterol and the Optimal Diet for Reducing Risk of Atherosclerosis." *Canadian Journal of Cardiology*, October 1995: pp. 123G-126G.

McNamara, Donald J. "Egg Consumption and Heart Disease Risk." *Nutrition Close-Up*, March 1996: p. 7.

Moore, Richard D. and Thomas A. Pearson. "Moderate Alcohol Consumption and Coronary Artery Disease." *Medicine*, July 1986: pp. 242-67.

Rimm, Eric B. et al. "Review of Moderate Alcohol Consumption and Reduced Risk of Coronary Heart Disease: Is the Effect Due to Beer, Wine, or Spirit?" *British Medical Journal*, March 1996: pp. 731-36.

Stehbens, William E. "Diet and Atherogenesis." *Nutrition Reviews*, January 1989: 1-12.

Thorley, Anthony. "Government Advice on Sensible Drinking Does Not Conflict with the Data." *British Medical Journal*, September 1996: pp. 624-25.

Chapter 8

"Dietary Choline and Synaptic Morphology in Mice." *Nutrition Reviews*, January 1987: pp. 25-7.

Lands, William E. M. "Alcohol and Energy Intake." *American Journal of Clinical Nutrition*, November 1995: pp. 1101S-6S.

Lieber, Charles S. "The Influence of Alcohol on Nutritional Status." *Nutrition Reviews*, July 1988: pp. 241-54.

Mitchell, Mack C. and H. Franklin Herlong. "Alcohol and Nutrition: Caloric Value, Bioenergetics, and Relationship to Liver Damage." *Annual Review Nutrition*, June 1986: pp. 457-74.

Whitney, Eleanor N. and Sharon R. Rolfes, *Understanding Nutrition*. Minneapolis/St. Paul: West Publishing Company, 1996. p. 287n.

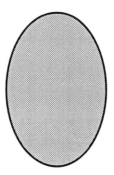

Index

YOU WILL ALSO WANT TO READ:

☐ **61157 I AM NOT A NUMBER!,** *by Claire Wolfe.* Thinking about going fishing? Enrolling your child in school? Getting a license to work as a plumber or hairdresser? Think again — because in the coming years, you won't be able to do any of the above without a federally issued ID number. In one of the most compelling works on personal freedom to date, author Claire Wolfe describes how the abuse of the Social Security number will erode privacy as your entire life can be accessed from a giant database — whether you want it there or not. The first step in stopping the "Numbers game," however, is to buy this book, before it's too late. *1998, 8½ x 11, 186 pp, soft cover.* $16.95.

☐ **94281 101 THINGS TO DO 'TIL THE REVOLUTION, Ideas and resources for self-liberation, monkey wrenching and preparedness,** *by Claire Wolfe.* We don't need a weatherman to know which way the wind blows — but we do need the likes of Claire Wolfe, whose book offers 101 suggestions to help grease the wheels as we roll towards the government's inevitable collapse. For the concerned citizen who wishes to keep a low profile, protect his or her rights, and survive in the "interesting times" which are sure to come, this is essential reading. *1996, 5½ x 8½, 216 pp, soft cover.* $15.95.

☐ **85203 STONED FREE, How to Get High Without Drugs,** *by Patrick Wells with Douglas Rushkoff.* Now you can just say "NO!" to drugs... and get high anyway! This book enumerates many drugless consciousness altering techniques, both timeless and recent in origin, that anyone can make use of. Meditation, breathing techniques, high-tech highs, sleep and dream manipulation, and numerous other methods are examined in detail. Avoid incarceration, save money, and skip the wear and tear on your body, while getting higher than a kite. *1995, 5½ x 8½, 157 pp, illustrated, soft cover.* $14.95.

☐ **14187 HOW TO LIVE WITHOUT ELECTRICITY — AND LIKE IT,** *by Anita Evangelista.* There's no need to remain dependent on commercial electrical systems for your home's comforts and security. This book describes many alternative methods that can help one become more self-reliant and free from the utility companies. Learn how to light, heat and cool your home, obtain and store water, cook and refrigerate food, and fulfill many other household needs without paying the power company! *1997, 5½ x 8½, 168 pp, illustrated, soft cover.* $13.95.

☐ **14176 HOW TO DEVELOP A LOW-COST FAMILY FOOD STORAGE SYSTEM,** *by Anita Evangelista.* If you're weary of spending a large percentage of your income on your family's food needs, then you should follow this amazing book's numerous tips on food-storage techniques. Slash your food bill by over fifty percent, and increase your self-sufficiency at the same time through alternative ways of obtaining, processing and storing foodstuffs. Includes methods of freezing, canning, smoking, salting, pickling, drying, and many other food-preservation procedures. *1995, 5½ x 8½, 120 pp, illustrated, indexed, soft cover.* $10.00.

☐ **14193 BACKYARD MEAT PRODUCTION,** *by Anita Evangelista.* If you're tired of paying ever-soaring meat prices, and worried about unhealthy food additives and shoddy butchering techniques, then you should start raising small meat-producing animals at home! You needn't live in the country, as most urban areas allow for this practice. This book clearly explains how to raise rabbits, chickens, quail, pheasants, guineas, ducks, and mini-goats and –pigs for their meat and by-products, which can not only be consumed but can also be sold or bartered to specialized markets. Improve your diet while saving money and becoming more self-sufficient! *1997, 5½ x 8½, 136 pp, illustrated, soft cover.* $14.95.

☐ **14178 THE WILD AND FREE COOKBOOK with a Special Roadkill Section,** *by Tom Squier.* Why pay top dollar for grocery-store food, when you can dine at no cost by foraging and hunting? Wild game, free of the steroids and additives found in commercial meat, is better for you, and many weeds and wild plants are more nutritious than the domestic fruits and vegetables found in the supermarket. Authored by a former Special Forces survival school instructor, this cookbook is chockfull of easy-to-read recipes that will enable your to turn wild and free food (including roadkill!) into gourmet meals. *1996, 7¼ x 11½, 306 pp, illustrated, indexed, soft cover.* $19.95.

☐ **14181 EAT WELL FOR 99¢ A MEAL,** *by Bill and Ruth Kaysing.* Want more energy, more robust, vigorous health? Then you must eat food that can impart these well-being characteristics and this book will be your faithful guide. As an important bonus, you will learn how to save lots of money and learn how to enjoy three homemade meals for a cost of less than one dollar per meal. This book will show you how to shop, stock your pantry, where to pick fresh foods for free, how to cook your 99¢ meal, what foods to grow yourself and more. *1996, 5½ x 8½, 204 pp, illustrated, indexed, soft cover.* $14.95.

☐ **14183 THE 99¢ A MEAL COOKBOOK,** *by Ruth and Bill Kaysing.* Ruth and Bill Kaysing have compiled these recipes with one basic thought in mind: people don't like over-processed foods and they can save a lot of money by taking these things into their own hands. These are practical recipes because they advise the cook where to find the necessary ingredients at low cost. And every bit as important — the food that you make will taste delicious! This is a companion volume to the *Eat Well For 99¢ A Meal.* Even in these days when the price of seemingly everything is inflated beyond belief or despair, 99¢ can go a long way toward feeding a person who is willing to save money by providing the labor for processing food. *1996, 5½ x 8½, 272 pp, indexed, soft cover.* $14.95.

To order any of the above titles, please use the order form below. If you are ordering with a Visa or MasterCard, you can call our toll-free number 1-800-380-2230, Monday through Friday, 8am to 4pm, Pacific Time. Check out our web site: www.loompanics.com

☐ **61157 I am Not a Number!, $16.95**

☐ **94281 101 Things to do 'Til the Revolution, $15.95**

☐ **14187 How To Live Without Electricity — And Like It, $13.95**

☐ **14176 How To Develop a Low-Cost Family Food-Storage System, $10.00**

☐ **14193 Backyard Meat Production, $14.95**

☐ **14178 The Wild & Free Cookbook, $19.95**

☐ **14181 Eat Well For 99¢ A Meal, $14.95**

☐ **14183 99¢ A Meal Cookbook, $14.95**

☐ **88888 1999 Main Catalog**
